I0692900

THE FUNCTION OF FREEDOM

MARGOT MONROE   DANIEL YOCOM

BLITHE ANDERSON   JOHN M. OLSEN

DANIELLE HARWARD   ELIZABETH SUGGS

MARIE TOLLSTRUP   J.E. ZARNOFSKY   C.H. LINDSAY

ALEXIS HANSEN   GRACE DIANE JESSEN

KAM HADLEY   CHRIS JONES   VALARIE SCHENK

ANNA BESSESEN   J. MILLIGAN   SARAH MURTAGH

JOHNNY WORTHEN   MIRANDA HUGHES

JAYROD P. GARRETT   CHRISTOPHER G. JONES

ERICA SWENSON   SHIRLEY MANNING

CARYN LARRINAGA   TIM HEARE   DENIS FEEHAN

CASSIDY WARD   RACHAEL BUSH   BRYAN YOUNG

The Function of Freedom
The League of Utah Writers 85th Anniversary Commemorative Anthology

Cover design © 2020 by the League of Utah Writers

Cover art: "Home of the Desert Rat" by Maynard Dixon

Edited by the Utah Freelance Editors Chapter of the League of Utah Writers

Formatted by FireDrake Designs | www.firedrakedesigns.com

Print ISBN: 978-0-9882367-9-0

Contents

Foreword

Welcome,

This humble collection of stories and poems has been made in celebration of the 85th anniversary of the League of Utah Writers. 1935-2020. It is a potpourri of ideas and styles from amateurs and professionals among our membership. It is an historical artifact and a souvenir for our 2020 Quills writing conference.

When considering ways to celebrate this august milestone, my idea for a mountain carving of the current president's grinning face was unfortunately vetoed by budget and time restraints. Instead we threw it open to the members, a call for submissions toward a book showcasing our skill and talent.

The subject could have been anything. We might have gone with something about time, endurance, creativity. The prompt itself, whatever it was, would be a starting place, a launch pad for ideas and expression.

We went with The Function of Freedom. This is a quote from the late great Toni Morrison; "The function of freedom is to free others." This we did to commemorate that great author's passing just last year, but also to challenge our writers to recognize their importance in culture and their place in history.

Not to put too sharp a point on it, but writers are the makers of history. Literally. Literally literally. We are the carriers of culture, the seeds for change, the imaginings of future shape. We are the record keepers and the therapists of an age. We focus thought and map the struggles of it. Whether we like it or not, we are reflections of our time and the weight of history presses on our minds and art until it is expressed by the crucible of words onto a page. Even in fiction, or perhaps, especially in fiction, the problems of our time are expressed and explored.

Big ideas. Those are the bones of our art. The smallest couplet, the silliest comedy, the grandest fantasy, each will have a germ of a big idea, if not a full-on sapling or... what's after sapling? Tree. A-full-on tree. These ideas will take root whether we like it or not, so why not plant one, an important one, a historic one, a favored one, a lovely one, and have our talented people grow that?

The Function of Freedom.

A seed. A start. A writing prompt. A collection of stories both timely and important. A celebration of writing, a look at the big idea.

As the front man for this grand organization, The League of Utah Writers, which is celebrating its 85th year of offering community, opportunity, and excellence to its members, I am proud to welcome you to our commemorative anthology wrestling—eternally—with the big ideas.

Johnny Worthen
President, League of Utah Writers

COMMUNITY
OPPORTUNITY
EXCELLENCE

Seattle Writer To Organize Utah Unit

SALT LAKE CITY, July 26—(AP) —Plans for the organization of local chapters of the League of Western Writers throughout Utah were announced here today by Miss Pamelia Pearl Jones of Seattle, secretary-treasurer of the organization.

She was organizing the state chapter here today.

The Ogden Standard-Examiner | July 26, 1935

A Brief History of the League of Utah Writers

As long as there have been humans in the Salt Lake Valley, Utah has been home to storytellers. Ancient people in this area told stories in petroglyphs and pictographs etched forever on cave walls. The Indigenous populations that settled called the valley home after that have a rich oral tradition of stories, tales and myths that made sense of the world and each other. When the Pioneers arrived, they brought the written word with them. The first public building they constructed was the Utah Theater, an acknowledgment of how important storytelling and entertainment was to the people of the frontier. Film-makers like Charlie Chaplin plied their trade here in the early days of cinema, entertaining Utah audiences with his first feature film in a one room movie palace on Main Street. Stories have always been a cornerstone of the culture of Utah and storytellers have been respected and revered for their ability in their craft.

It makes sense that Utah would give rise to an organization dedicated to advancing the art of letters and storytelling.

The story of the League of Utah Writers begins as the country was awakening from the sleep of the Great Depression and art was something people could once more pay attention to.

On July 26, 1935, Pamelia Pearl Jones, the treasurer of the League of Western Writers, traveled to Utah from her home in Seattle to found a chapter for the Beehive state. In those days, organizations of craftspeople were common, but many faded out. The League of Western Writers didn't last long under that name, but it left an enduring legacy on the storytellers of Utah.

In 1939, as World War II sparked across Europe, The League of Utah Writers solidified its position as a stronghold of the written word in the state. Under the direction of Frank C. Robertson, the writers of Utah gathered at the Art Barn in Salt Lake City and formally transformed from a chapter of the League of Western Writers into the League of Utah Writers. The organization absorbed a couple of other writing groups into their fold, including the local chapter of the League of American Penwomen and the Blue Quill Writers, a still-active chapter that predates the League itself by almost a decade.

Across most of the next century, the League fashioned itself as a bastion of support for writers across the state. Immediately, they began holding conferences, known then as Roundups, to teach each other the craft of assembling letters into effective stories. In 1938, the first president of the League, Olive Burt, added to the conferences the tradition of the Poet's Breakfast, offering a place for poets to practice their skills, learn from keynote speakers, and enjoy a Sunday brunch. Guests of these Roundups ranged from Louis L'Amour and Mary Higgins Clark to Tracy Hickman and Terry Brooks. These bestselling writers, editors, and agents of international renown were gathered in Utah to advance the careers of Utah writers and to teach their trade. The Roundups traveled the state, north and south, until finally settling in Salt Lake City.

The tradition of annual writing conferences held by the League continues with this, our 85th conference. In 2018, the name of the conferences were changed from the "Roundup" to "Quills." The theme of the 85th conference is "Community, Opportunity, Excellence."

I can't think of three words that better exemplify our history.

As the League Historian for the last year, it's been my great pleasure to wade into the history of the League and piece together the personalities who have made this organization flourish over the years. I've been able to put together fragments of our history and gain a window into what the essence of storytelling in our state has been for the last eight-and-a-half decades. As we look ahead, I'm excited to see what comes from our organization. What writers will we nurture into stardom? What future bestsellers hide among our ranks?

By dedicating ourselves to our community and craft, it's only a matter of time and I can't wait to see that history happen before my very eyes.

Bryan Young
Historian, League of Utah Writers

Clubs Gain Insight Into Factory Work

The Blue Quill club and Rays club made a tour Tuesday of the following manufacturing plants: Continental Baking company, Quinn Garment company, Shupe-Williams Candy company, Weber Central Dairy association, Ogden Utah Knitting company, Grossenbach Hat company and Midwestern Dairy Products company.

The Blue Quill members obtained information for stories for trade journals, other magazines and newspapers.

At the Weber Central dairy the writers were much interested in seeing the processes used in manufacturing powdered milk and operation of churns that make 1300 pounds of butter at a time. At noon, the managers of the Weber Centray dairy served a lunch to both clubs.

The Blue Quill club will visit other plants in Ogden in the near future.

The Ogden Standard-Examiner | June 6, 1934

Past Presidents of the League of Utah Writers

1935-1939: Olive W. Burt
1939-1941: Frank C. Robertson
1942-1943: Carlton Culmsee
1944-1945: Cleone Montgomery
1946-1947: Martha C. Wright
1948-1949: Willard C. Luce
1950-1951: Mable Harmer
1952-1953: Frank C. Robertson
1954-1955: Carlton Culmsee
1956-1957: Edward T. Tuttle
1958-1959: Theron H. Luke
1960-1961: Mary K. Knowles
1962-1963: Cameron Johns
1964-1965: Delillie S. Sanford
1966-1967: June F. Krambule
1968-1969: Bonnie L. Emmertson
1970-1971: Betty G. Spencer
1972-1973: Wanda B. Blaisedell
1974-1975: Caroline Eyering Miner
1976-1977: Clarence Socwell and Dora Flack

1978-1979: Esther Phelps Parks
1979-1980: Jean R. Poulson
1980-1981: Arlene Hamblin
1981-1982: Brenda Bensch
1982-1983: Sally T. Taylor
1983-1984: Helen Mar Cook
1984-1985: Dorothy Farnell
1985-1986: Thaya Davis Char
1986-1987: Louise Hurd
1987-1988: Wanda Peterson
1988-1989: Richard Tice
1989-1990: Ruth Harris Swaner
1990-1991: Ana Baker Marcusen
1991-1993: Norbert G. Bensch
1993-1994: Vera Bakker
1994-1995: LuAnn Brobst
1996-1997: Marcia Anstead
1997-1998: Marcia Ford
1998-1999: Bettyanne Gillette
1999-2000: Carole Cole
2000-2001: Dorothy Crofts
2001-2002: Carolyn Campbell
2002-2003: Charlene Hirschi
2003-2004: Kathy Jones
2004-2005: Becky Crum
2005-2006: DeLoa Sharp
2006-2007: Andy Anderson
2007-2008: Marilyn Richardson
2008-2009: Natalie Pace
2009-2010: Mike Eldredge
2010-2011: Edwin Smith
2011-2012: Tim Keller
2012-2013: Irene Hastings
2013-2014: Emily Younker

2014-2015: Amanda Luzzader
2015-2016: Chris Miller
2016-2018: Jared Quan
2018-2020: Johnny Worthen
2020-Present: John M. Olsen

Content Warning

This collection includes stories, poems, and personal essays that contain:

- kidnapping
- genocide and the Holocaust
- substance abuse
- sexual and physical assault
- child abuse
- loss of parent/spouse
- end of life
- PTSD
- guns
- murder/death
- drowning

THE FUNCTION OF
FREEDOM

DNR

Margot Monroe

S hort of tattooing "DNR or I will haunt the ever-loving fuck out of you" to her sternum, she doesn't see how she could have avoided this situation. She is fairly certain her husband wouldn't have honored a Living Will anyway.

He slumps onto her bed, pressing his face to the bleached white sheets. Her hand—the one without the IV port—is against his mouth and the crown of his head presses into her hip.

"I can't do this. I can't do this without you."

Well, no shit. She'd told him that years ago but she managed everything anyway. And now here he is, asking *her* for more.

She misses folding her arms. She would put her weight on her back foot and give him the *look*. Instead, she's behind him, watching this scene of *spousal devotion*, all this emotion without a way to express it.

He repeats his inadequacies to her hand, mumbling again and again like his incompetence could summon her.

To his credit, it had worked before. "Oh, you fill the dish-washer better than I do." And when he "tried," he loaded the dishes so a Cheerio always got baked into the side of the bowl. Maybe it would have been less work in the long run to make him learn to do it properly.

Then again, there is no long run. It's not her problem anymore.

Her body had been in this ICU room for the past week and a half. She could only imagine the horror show her house would be. By now, every bowl would be encrusted with Cheerio barnacles.

One morning at brunch, one of her friends had said, "You know, I think if I died, Paul would be remarried within a year." The general consensus up and down the table, both that Paul would remarry so quickly and their own husbands too, should have been shocking. Then, one of their other girlfriends said, "But if something happened to Nick, I wouldn't get remarried. I mean, he's the best man I ever found but . . . he's . . . well . . . Nicky." The Bloody Mary and mimosa glasses clinked in agreement. It wasn't that they didn't love their husbands; entrenched gender roles and disappointment just had a way of killing romance.

He was heartbroken, and rightfully, but her patience had reached its limit and her sympathy was exhausted. It wasn't "I need you." It wasn't "I want to get old with you." It was "I can't figure out how to care for our son since I never bothered to learn in the first place."

The ventilator's whirr sounds like quick short waves coming in. If only she could ride one out to sea.

They'd talked about their end of life wishes. That she wouldn't want to be kept alive on a machine. That this was her nightmare.

The doctor had examined her body then said she had suffered a devastating and irreversible stroke. She wonders if her husband had done CPR when he found her.

That part was a bit murky.

The damnedest thing. She'd been cleaning the kitchen, singing along to *Les Misérables* and about to proclaim herself Jean Valjean. She'd been off all morning, fatigued and exhausted and maybe getting sick? She cleaned the kitchen as quickly as possible to forestall the utter disaster of her husband caring for the house. But she sang, "*Who am I? Who am I? I'm Jean Vajah.*" And despite knowing she could and her brain telling her mouth how to say it, she could not.

Darkness took her. She woke up disoriented. It felt like resting her eyes for ten minutes after work, then waking at dusk in a panic because she thought she'd slept through the night.

Waking up without a body was similarly unsettling. She could hear and see and smell just fine. And she never stopped seeing, even at night. She missed the quiet calm of closed eyes. The only physical sensations were the warmth of sunshine and trying to leave the confines of the hospital building. The hospital boundary pushed like two magnets with the same polarities. The harder she pushed, the more it repelled her.

She'd watched the MRI, her soulless body going in and out of the machine. The neurologist gave her husband the results: no brain activity. She couldn't get better and she'd never wake up. Her husband asked for an EEG after that. The EEG results also showed no brain activity. She couldn't tell if he believed the neurologist, but at least he stopped asking for more tests.

She'd have told him he was throwing good money after bad. And every penny spent on her medical care is one penny less for her family to live on. All this care, just to keep her body alive: tubes and hand sanitizer and certified nurse's aides and . . .

He stops addressing her hand and stands up to kiss her forehead. He pushes the chair back against the wall and stands at her bedside.

"I'll see you tomorrow."

He'd never shown half this much enthusiasm for her

before. He'd certainly never dropped anything, even when she asked for help.

"But, babe, what would the guys think about you if I canceled on them like that? They think you're cool."

But now here he is. Neglecting everything in his life to sit and mumble to her hand.

Or maybe that's what he always wanted? To *look* productive without having to do anything? She'd ask for help and he'd say no like he was doing her a favor.

Perhaps she was like oxygen, just there until it wasn't. And that was the only way he could notice—when he was gasping and breathless.

She realized he'd never volunteer to be her oxygen and so she found her own. Her work, her friends, time with her son. She could either look at taking him to his jiu-jitsu lesson as *one more errand* or she could sign herself up. Their quality time together was her favorite oxygen. From his practice driving on his way to the studio, to sparring with him, to almost reaching her brown belt.

She never thought something she enjoyed so much would kill her. It's not like jiu-jitsu was cigarettes or scotch. But she took a hard tumble and the bruise on the side of her calf was worse than she'd thought. A clot broke off. Stroke.

He hunches over to kiss her forehead. The tube in her mouth is in his way, as is the NG tube down her nose feeding her.

Rage rushes through her. She misses the flush of heat that crawls up her fingers and her heartbeat ringing in her ears. All of the gritty, physical manifestations of emotion. The simple creature comforts of being a creature.

She flings herself at her body, trying to get back in. Desperate to tell him how badly he'd fucked up and to protect her son. She sinks right through it, coming through on the other side.

He clears his throat and she faces him over her body. "I don't know how to do this without you. I'm sorry. I should have taken him to his lesson."

That would have deprived her of cherished jiu-jitsu time. He really didn't know her.

"I'll see you tomorrow. And I'll have a surprise for you." Then he whispers "I love you" into her hair.

This does nothing to appease her. She longs for the bunching of her shoulders, the way the muscles in her right temple would clench. If he loved *her* he wouldn't have done this to her. Her brain is irrevocably broken, and here he was asking for the impossible

His *I love you*? Who was that for? Certainly not her. It felt performative. The doctors told him she isn't in there anymore. He should be taking care of the life and family they'd built by being there for their son.

At almost sixteen, he is old enough to go into the ICU, but he hadn't visited and for that she is grateful. She doesn't want him to remember her like this.

He doesn't *need* constant supervision and caretaking, but he needs someone. Who is with him now while her husband spends long hours at her side?

Her body would only atrophy. But their son? He's a growing boy needing guidance and care. Not solitude after losing his mother.

Her husband finally huffs and walks out the door. She follows him. The only time she can see outside is when the doors open. The windows turned opaque in the hospital. Sunlight streams in and the sensation of warmth spreads through her, but that's it.

She watches a spring drizzle, the drops making the daffodil buds bob. The daffodil buds are yellow at the tip. The tulips have only grown leaves so far. It's a bookstore and latte afternoon with this rain. Instead, she's stuck here.

Jealousy of the outside world mounts, and she wanders the hospital in a sulk. She settles in behind another patient to read a House of Windsor scandal in their *Us Weekly*. She's curious to read more when she is irresistibly towed away.

Fear without a bodily response is likewise unsettling. There's no uptick in heart rate, no rush of power and strength as adrenaline floods her. Only naked fear.

She uses doorways like a civilized person, but she is dragged through walls and people. Happily, it's dark inside. The last thing she needs is to gawk at someone's innards.

She's jerked outside as her gurney rolls toward the ambulance. For the moments her body is outside, she is too. She would give anything to feel raindrops land in her hair. She peers at the daffodils, pleased that life marches on despite her situation. She revels in the signs of spring until she's tugged into the ambulance.

Maybe they are carting her off to harvest her organs?

That's a happy thought. What gifts she could give. A heart and kidneys, liver, bone and cartilage. What a joy if she could end so much suffering, both hers and the recipients'.

Her emotions shift easily without the physiological. No hormones to metabolize in her brain, telling her happy or sad or angry. No heart rate to contend with, just transitory emotions.

Until the ambulance slows. The gurney lurches as the ambulance stops.

Then she remembers her husband said, "See you tomorrow," not "Goodbye." She probably isn't at the organ harvesting plant. Not that those are a thing. Probably. She would never be that lucky anyway.

The doors swing open on a long-term care facility. It's not nice but it won't be on the news for shocking elder abuse either.

She's jerked outside for one wholesome, overwhelming

moment. Raindrops splatter her soulless body, making grey circles on the white linens. Tiny bright green buds on the maple trees flank the doors. The world is waking up while she's in stasis.

Before she can take any sort of metaphorical breath, they tug her into the building.

She hates it. The long-term care facility is smaller than the hospital, and the likelihood of anything besides watching TV is low.

She settles in the sunlight near the table, watching them move her body and all of its accompanying tubes to the bed.

She finally sees the bruise on her calf. It's a mixture of green and yellow mottling. Funny something so simple could do this to her.

And now, she'll watch over her body and the residents like a useless gargoyle, frustrated, angry, and powerless.

She has no desire to explore the facility. She is certain there's no one like her.

Hell, she'd take the physical manifestations of depression at this point. The exhaustion and numbness. The lack of hunger and the messy house. She'd take any of that over this bland existence.

She has no eyes to shut. She can't watch the stars wheel overhead through the windows. There is nothing but stasis.

But the sun comes up and she learns the daily noises of the nursing home as they filter in.

Everything shatters with familiar sounds from the doorway.

"Dad . . . I . . ."

He brought their son? That motherfucker brought her boy to see her like this? *This* is her surprise?

"Just go talk to her."

"But *that* isn't Mom. She isn't in there anymore."

"That," her husband points to the body in the bed, "is your mother."

"Not anymore. Mom wouldn't like this and you know it." His nostrils flared. "We filled out my learner's permit application, and I wasn't sure about the organ donor stuff. And she said—" He clears his throat once, then squares his shoulders. "She said the *only* reason she'd want to be on life support was so her organs could be donated. That life support was to support *life*. And organ donation was about life. Mom would absolutely hate this."

"Don't say that."

Their son folds his arms, looking at the bed.

Her poor boy has to argue to turn off his mother's life support. Overwhelming grief washes her away. At this point, her chest would be tight and angry tears would simmer behind her face. She is utterly powerless and can only watch her family stand around the bed.

"Dad, let's go," the son says. "I can't see her like this. It hurts too much."

Her husband looks like he thinks about arguing, then says, "Okay." He leans forward and kisses her body's forehead. "I'll see you tomorrow."

There is no describing the anger of the perfectly powerless. She wants to hit him or kick him, anything to make this senseless torment stop.

She hovers around her son, wishing she could hold or protect him. Tell him how sorry she is for what happened. She couldn't do anything but hope he had *enough*.

Enough time with her. Enough strength and ingenuity to make his way in life. Enough resilience. He was her life's work. And she didn't regret a moment of it.

A dreadful monotony takes over as she returns to her room.

She hovers near the floor, in the corner, by the table, where sunlight falls from the window.

Within the next couple weeks, she gets dragged along to the hospital for a tracheotomy for her ventilator and a port in her stomach so they can feed her more easily.

The care of her body horrifies her. They clean up after her menses. The way her hair grows and greys and gets tied back. Her unruly eyebrows. She wasn't vain in life, but her appearance matches her emotional state.

Nothing but the daily routine of catheters and feeding tubes and hand sanitizer and a despised husband sitting vigil.

Until one day her son comes back. The days had blended together, but she guesses it's been about six months since she saw him last. He's grown and so has his hair. She wonders if her husband would even notice and ask him to get a haircut. She would guess he's still practicing jiu-jitsu from the loose, confident way he walks and moves.

The aide leads him to her room and pulls out the chair for him.

"How are you?" the aide asks gently.

Her son bites his lips. If she had a heart, it would break seeing him do that. She immediately hovers around him.

"She didn't want this." He looks at her body's face and shakes his head. "She was healthy and alive, now she's on machines. She'll never get better."

The aide looks out the door, then back to her son. "I will say this only once. If you tamper with *any* of this medical equipment, there will be legal ramifications."

She's angry and afraid for what might happen if he should make any rash, but right, decisions.

"I couldn't do that to my father."

Pride and sadness. Two very different emotions, coexisting and swirling through her. It isn't a sensation she cares for.

She wouldn't worry about his resilience. Well, of course she would because she's his mother. But he knows himself and what's right.

The aide nods and says, "If you need anything, there's a pull cord. I'll check back shortly." She gestures to the string hanging from the wall then steps out.

Her boy sits in the chair next to the bed and looks at her. Emotions flicker over his face, from a terrible longing to anger, finally settling on sadness.

"Dad says I'm supposed to talk to you. I don't know what the fuck to say."

It's the first time she's heard him say "fuck," but the situation warrants it.

He leans forward, putting a hand on the bed, but not touching her. She can't blame him for that. This mother facsimile is a lot to handle.

"I miss you. I hate to say it would be easier if . . . if he'd just made the right choice and . . . pulled the Band-Aid. He can't move on and I'm . . ." His voice chokes. "He still has this fucking idea that you'll wake up." He wipes at his nose and sniffles. "But that's fucking ludicrous because, a) you'd kill him for doing this to you and, b) you're not even in there.

"I remember the summer I'd skinned my knee and wouldn't pull the Band-Aid off. You got so frustrated that you snapped, 'It's a goddamn Band-Aid and pussyfooting around won't make it any easier. Just goddamn do it, goddamn.'" His laughter turns real as he remembers. "I couldn't believe you would even say that to me. I'm sorry I can't do that for our family"

He sighs, stands, and pushes the chair back to the wall.

"I can't handle Dad at home. I figure I'll do my homework here. It's not like he helps."

Hating her husband more is impossible.

He sits at the table and works on his homework.

The aide returns.

"How are things?" she asks.

He shrugs.

"Are you thirsty? Soda or orange juice or anything?"

"Could I get some orange juice, please?"

The aide smiles at his "please." She nods and steps out the door.

"I'm guessing you don't need anything," he says, addressing the body in the bed. "Because if you did, you would have it by now."

He turns back to his homework and says, "I was real mad for a while, I mean, sometimes I still am. Dad is just . . . I don't know. I want to say he's trying, but he does this weird 'my wife is in a coma' thing. That he has to come and visit you." He snorts. "He's been doing it for the last seven months without you. Well, no. *I've* been doing it. He likes to act like he has. He can't even manage to clean the lint out of the goddamn dryer."

The aide comes back in with a paper box of orange juice. She hands him the carton, then checks the body in the bed.

"Thank you. She's not in pain, is she?"

The aide shakes her head, but it morphs into a shrug. "Sometimes she makes signs of discomfort, and we take care of her."

"What hurts her?"

"She'll get bed sores sometimes, despite the mattress and everything. She still gets her menses, so she gets cramps. Stuff like that."

His anger flares. "*This* isn't my mother. You've turned my mother's body into a zombie. He was wrong to do this."

"That may be, but this is the situation we have." The aide finishes her ministrations and turns back to the boy.

He makes a frustrated noise and turns to his homework. "Thank you. I know. I just . . . I'll come around more." The aide smiles and leaves.

She can't decide if this delights or terrifies her. She gets to see her son! But only because this cinder-block bunker is better than home.

A timer goes off on his phone and he gathers his things. He stands at the bedside and says, "I gotta go. I thought about quitting jiu-jitsu, but it makes me think of how much fun we had. Then, sometimes I wonder if I wouldn't have wanted jiu-jitsu lessons, you'd still be here. But I can't talk to Dad about this, you know? I just . . . if it's my fault, I'm sorry."

She would give anything to tell him it wasn't his fault.

He rubs a hand over his face and says, "I'll be back later. I just miss you so much." He leans forward, like he considers kissing her forehead, but rocks back instead, slinging his backpack on.

Her husband comes in fifteen minutes after her son leaves. Maybe she's been so checked out she hadn't noticed, but he looks like shit. His face is haggard and his hair is greasy. He's gained weight and his stained clothing accentuates it. She would give anything for her friend's prediction to come true and her husband to remarry. She didn't realize how much she would like that stability for her family. Her poor boy, living like this.

A white-hot distillation of anger swells within her, but without the physiological component, it's hard to maintain and fades.

She slinks back to her sunshine in the corner.

The only bright spot of her existence over the next few years is watching her son grow into a man. He brings prom pictures and report cards and college acceptance letters. It's the only thing that makes her feel a little bit human. These disembodied years have torn at the fabric of her being, destroying any sense of humor or grace that remained.

When he leaves for school, she gets the whole empty nester experience and the only thing punctuating her days are her husband's visits.

Unexpectedly, her son comes in when he's supposed to be away at school and sits next to the bed.

"I shouldn't have left," he says, addressing the body in the bed. He purses his lips and runs his hands through his hair. "I thought he'd be okay, I really did. I'm so sorry, Mom." He makes a choking noise, then gathers himself. "The house burned down." Tears slip from his eyes and he swipes at them, then clears his throat.

She longs to shelter him from the hardships of the world.

"The Fire Marshall thinks it started in the laundry room." He bows his head. "I was only gone for six months. And he couldn't manage it. He couldn't take care of me and I understood that. But he couldn't take care of himself either."

He finally reaches out and holds her pallid hand. It's the first time he's touched her body in years. It had been years since she'd even thought about trying to get back into her body and now it is all she wants. A chance to hold her son's hand and give or take any sort of comfort.

"Since I can make your medical decisions now, I'm going to have them turn it all off." He bows his head to her hand. "I'm sorry it took so long for me to do this. Not that—" Another choking noise. "Not that I wanted Dad to die, but . . ."

Anger flares through her, that her husband just got to die without experiencing years of purgatory. It's quickly washed away by tenderness for her son.

"I've missed you so much, and now I can think about how it used to be. When we'd do jiu-jitsu together. I still can't believe the day you went 'fuck it' and threw me." He laughs, once, setting down her hand and wiping his eyes. "I always knew you were there to take care of me. And everything you taught me? That kept me going. It was enough." He picks up her hand again and holds it in both of his.

"Maybe planning both of your funerals at the same time isn't the best plan, but . . . Dad left when you did anyway.

"Sometimes, I pretend you're here. But I don't want that for you. You'd hate it. I wouldn't keep you trapped here just for my imagination."

He stands up, setting her hand on her stomach.

"I'm getting the doctors."

Perhaps the years had been as difficult for her husband as they had been for her. He had the *choice* to do the right thing, but not the strength.

He leaves the room and she hovers over her body. Her body hasn't had anything approaching a *life* in this bed, but there are new wrinkles and the hair around her face is so grey. The undertaker will have a hell of a time making her look presentable.

He comes back with a medical team.

"Are you sure?" the doctor says. "Are we waiting for anyone else?"

"There's no one else I want here. She never wanted this."

"You shouldn't make this decision under duress."

Her son shakes his head. "She never wanted this. I decided a long time ago this would be the first thing to do when my dad died."

He signs all the necessary forms. She is proud her son is the man she hoped he could be. She hates that he'll be alone in the world, that he had to make these decisions, but relief washes over her. This waking hell can be over. A fresh wave of curiosity overtakes her. What comes next?

They remove the ventilator tube from the tracheotomy port.

Her son sits next to the bed, holding her hand. Tears stream down his face.

The chest of her body hitches, but the breath doesn't come. She stays next to her son, gratitude and grief warring.

A relaxing and releasing begin at the edges of her existence. Like taking off shapewear and washing her face after a fancy event. An exhalation and relief to just *be*.

"Goddamn, I'm sorry it took so long to do this."

The colors in the room desaturate. The whites turn grey, then black.

It is the first time she's experienced true darkness since the stroke.

And, like the leading edge of a mudslide, the first pebbles tumble down the slope, quickly followed by utter darkness and oblivion.

His heart, despite the grief, is lighter than it's been in years. He walks out of the long-term care facility, blinking in the springtime sun.

MARGOT MONROE (Salt City Genre Writers) is a romance writer living in Salt Lake City with her husband, daughter, two Italian Greyhounds and a flock of black-capped chickadees and lesser goldfinches in her backyard. She's the Writing Coordinator for the Salt City Genre Writers chapter of the League of Utah Writers. You can find her on Twitter @gowritemargot.

Blue Quill Club Is Entertained by 2 Utah Writers

The Blue Quill club was delightfully entertained on Thursday evening when guest night was held at the auditorium of the Utah Power & Light company. President Tom Livingood presided. Harrison R. Merrill, professor of journalism at the Brigham Young university at Provo, and former editor of the Improvement Era, and Frank C. Robertson, of Springville, noted author of western stories, were the guest speakers, who were presented by Miss Helen Hinckley.

Mr. Merrill spoke on writing of verse and the story from the viewpoints of the editor and the writer. He expressed the hope that Utah would produce at some time an author that would rank with Zane Gray in depicting the lives of its people. Mr. Robertson, who is a regular contributor to magazines that feature western stories and the author of seven entertaining novels on the western theme, spoke of slanting the writing to the editor and the reader. About 100 guests were present. Frank Francis of News and Views was a special guest. A musical program was also given. Miss Jeannette Morrell played a piano solo and songs were given by a girls' chorus under the direction of Elda Blackburn.

After the meeting a no-host supper was given at Keeley's cafe. Those present were Mr. and Mrs. Merrill, Frank C. Robertson, Mr. and Mrs. Tom Livingood, Mrs. Mary Ek Knowles, Mrs. Naoma Garrison, Mrs. Leona Engstrom McCune, Miss Helen Hinckley, Ben Carter, Mrs. Ada Hurst Brown, Mrs. Drucilla McFarland, Miss Mary Peterson, Mrs. Fava K. Parker, Mrs. Ivy Williams Stone, and daughter Josephine, Mrs. Grace Peterson, Mrs. Lorene K. Bleecker, Mrs. Lella M. Hoggan, Mrs. Marie J. Maher, Mrs. Blanche Kendell McKey and Mrs. Eva Willes Wangsgard. Mrs. Bleecker was in charge of the supper.

The Ogden Standard-Examiner | April 26, 1936

Hometown

Daniel Yocom

G ail took a couple of deep breaths and wiped her sweaty palms on her Levis. She couldn't hear the motorcycles yet, but they were coming. They were coming from the south, and nothing good had come from the south since the end of the war.

Too many modern cowboys were trying to make their own kingdoms out there. Eventually one would lose, then push out to try again elsewhere. Hometown had dealt with those who had wanted to rebuild their egos.

The birds' chirping faded to nothing and everything went quiet. Gail's fingernails dug in between the grains of wood on the arms of the chair. Damn. Her knuckles refused to loosen. She stretched her back and neck muscles. She steadied her breathing. Birds sang spring songs again. She listened and allowed the sound to sooth her muscles until she could stretch her fingers.

She had just settled her chair when Nancy signaled from the rooftop across the street—nineteen. Spotters sent word earlier in the morning about unknown motorcycle travelers. Word spread and most of the townspeople had hunkered down to see what would happen. The streets were left for Gail and her deputies.

Standing, she assessed the street. Her focus was sharp as she took in the details of the damaged buildings, the movement of birds, and the rat that scurried in front of the building Nancy was on. The adrenaline rush was an addiction and a curse. The flow had never been as great as the last battle of San Jose, but that was death for those who didn't make it. Her muscles tightened and mental exercises kicked in. She would store the energy until it was needed.

In front of an old convenience store, now the general store, the shadow crept back toward her. There was no shade on the broken pavement. Just the sidewalk lining the front of the building. Gail stretched again and remembered what it was like to have large parks with fields of grass. Couldn't waste water like that anymore. Hell, they couldn't waste it on the small section on the side of the building where there was a picnic table. Only a few clumps of grass grew with the weeds. All of it already turning brown on the edges and dying like everything else.

The rumble of engines echoed off the brick structures. Working motorized vehicles weren't seen much anymore, and that sound worked better than any warnings or gunshots to get any stragglers off the streets.

She checked her gun to make sure there was a round in the chamber. She slipped it back in the holster and set it on the chair. She positioned it so she could grab the weapon if needed. Her combat knife settled in the small of her back.

Gail was about to play another crazy game of chicken.

The bikers moved slowly down the street, just fast enough to keep them upright. Their heads were swinging from side to side and up and down as they watched the buildings. They were no strangers to the risk they took riding down the main street. A pickup built from parts and different makes brought up the end. A young man riding single led the group. He saw Gail and swung his bike into the parking lot in front of her.

The leader rode up and calmly turned off the motor. Most of the bikes followed him into the lot but stayed near the street, giving the two of them lots of room. The truck with four bikes stationed around it stayed on the road. Gail took it in as they glanced back and forth from her to their surroundings.

They carried a lot of weapons, but their hands were empty and kept in sight. The leader wore the remains of an army shirt with ribbons. He was too young to have them. Damn. Gail rubbed her chin to let Nancy know something was amiss. She balanced her stance and put her fists on her hips.

The leader spoke. "Hi, we've been on the road a long time." He climbed off his bike to stand beside it. "It has been days since we've seen other people." He took a couple of steps forward.

"And, what makes you think you should be stopping here?" Gail's muscles twitched with anticipation. The whole scene immediately imprinted. The leader stopped, several of the other riders dropped their gaze, and four rifles eased out over the ledges on the opposite rooftops. The rat was gone.

"We were hoping to, well, if you would barter for supplies, that would be enough." He took another step closer and extended his hand. "My name is Doug."

Gail moved with the precision of years in the field. She clasped Doug's extended wrist with her left hand and rolled. His head thumped on the sidewalk. She came up with her knee on his chest and his right arm extended out behind her. In her right hand was the knife; it rested with its blade between his legs.

His face was all scrunched up, and tears leaked from the sides of his eyes. Some of the other bikers had shifted, but nobody reached for a weapon or moved closer. Something about this gang wasn't right, but the game of chicken was still on since they hadn't turned away.

She spoke loudly so she could be heard by all the bikers. "Now let's have a little chat. First, I want everyone to know that with one small flick of my wrist I can sever an artery, and your leader will bleed out before anyone can get here to stop it."

Doug's left hand raised, patted the air, and settled back down to the cement.

"Good start. You ain't old enough for those ribbons you're wearing. So, what the hell are you doing having them on your chest?"

"I didn't earn them, but they're mine." Doug was blinking. "My brother gave them to me before his last deployment."

"And?"

"He was heading to the Philippines. Odds were he wasn't going to return, and he didn't."

Gail shuddered. She'd lost good friends there.

"I don't mean any disrespect, but most people don't know what a ribbon means, and they have allowed us some safe passage over the past months. And, just because I didn't serve doesn't mean we don't know how to fight."

"Where you from?"

"I'm from San Diego. The rest are from all over the Southwest. Even a couple of us are from Mexico."

"The Southwest went through rough times. Horror stories come out of there. If you're talking the truth, then you've seen your share of action, no matter what you were doing before Hell was unleashed."

"Yes, and we made it here." His blinking became a stare. He wasn't resisting the hold, but he was still tensed up for a fight.

"'How' becomes the real question then. Who did you pledge to?"

"Didn't. None of us did."

"You telling me you didn't pledge colors with all that artillery you're packing?" Gail could see some of the riders were shifting their weight.

Footsteps came up behind Gail. The out-of-rhythm steps of the prosthetic leg identified Robert, the town's mayor. "It looks like you have this well under control, Sheriff."

"Yes, Bob, I think we do. What the hell are you doing here?"

Robert moved forward to the edge of the sidewalk so he was standing where Gail could see him and still watch the crowd in the parking lot. He held up his left arm to everyone since he wasn't wearing his right one. He had lost most of his right side but pulled through. "Good morning, or, maybe, good afternoon everyone. I'm Mayor Robert Guthrie."

Gail didn't want to spend any time on Robert's normal grandstanding while there were this many new guns sitting in a parking lot of Hometown.

"As you can tell, our town is well protected. But we are a poor place, nothing worthy of stealing."

Doug started to talk until Gail pressed the flat of her blade against his leg.

Robert glanced down at Doug and continued talking to all of them. "We don't even have enough to build a jail. You see, we decided we didn't need a jail because there is a lot of open land out there, and if you are planning trouble, you can leave. If you create trouble, there is plenty of room for another grave. No, we don't have time for that either. There are plenty of coyotes and buzzards out there. Anyway, our sheriff and her deputies protect our town and manage our jail."

Those gathered in the lot exchanged nervous looks as Robert turned his back on them. He spoke over his shoulder as he limped into the store. "The sheriff has final decision if you can stay in town or need to move on."

Damn stupid of him. Several hands dropped to their sides, out of sight.

"We don't want trouble." Doug almost barked out the words. He was loud, and Gail jumped a little.

He spoke more calmly as he looked up at her, "We don't. If you want us to leave, we'll just go. But we don't have much food nor water. Maybe just another day or two." She could feel his muscles tense then relax.

"Is that all you're looking for?"

"Not really, but we understand." Doug let out a long, slow breath.

"What then?"

"I think we are like you, looking for a place to start over." He rolled his head to the side and looked at the people he rode in with. "We might know how to fight, but we don't want to. We fought to survive. If we can survive without fighting, that would be better."

"Ain't never seen anyone surviving the Southwest without pledging and fighting."

"And I haven't heard of any who came out of the military and didn't start running their own gang. But you act like military, and that knife and gun are military issue."

Gail stared him down for a moment before he continued.

"My brother had the same gear."

Damn. He was pulling at her emotions, and this was no time to allow that.

"There are some who really need to stay. Will you let them?"

"What?" The question caught Gail off guard. She let go of his hand and held her palm out. "Who?"

Doug didn't say anything. He waved his arm and Gail watched as most of the bikers turned their heads to look back at the truck. The door opened and two young women climbed out of the cab. Each of them holding the tiny bundle of a baby.

"Don't know if they can make it to the next town. Don't know if we will. But, will you let them stay?"

Gail stood and took a step back from the man on the sidewalk. Of all of the fucking crap. "Who're the fathers?"

"Don't know. Probably dead or we ran them off. We rescued those two just under a year ago from a small gang outside L.A. If David hadn't been an ER nurse, don't know if the little ones would be here now. In fact, a number of us wouldn't be."

"You have a doctor?" Gail was losing control of the situation as the implications mounted.

"No. But, he knows a lot that has kept us alive."

Gail stepped back and sat down on her chair. She jumped, then picked up her gun and set it on her lap as she resettled.

"You really survived the Southwest to bring expectant mothers out?"

Doug slipped one hand under his head to rub where it had hit the cement. "It was the right thing to do. We've lost more friends than we've found along the way. But, yeah, we decided to get out and find a place. If not for all of us, at least for them."

"Holy shit." Gail saw Nancy and someone else standing with their guns held in front of them, ready. She signaled she was okay.

"You have other skills in your group, I mean, beside a medic?" Gail was no longer watching Doug. He talked while she looked at the faces of the people in the parking lot. Some were daring to smile a little at each other. There were a couple of women who leaned forward and hugged the shoulders of the men they were riding with. Doug was still talking when she held up her hand, which still had her knife in it.

He stopped talking and everything went quiet except for one of the babies crying.

"Everybody, put down any weapons you're carrying and walk away from the bikes to the other side of the parking lot, over by that bad wall." She looked down at Doug as she signaled her deputies to collect the weapons. "This is a trial basis. The Mayor's words are true--we don't have a jail. It's rough here, but better than the desert."

Gail stood again and extended her hand to Doug. She pulled him to his feet and caught him before he fell down from loss of balance.

"I fought," she said "I've seen a lot of death and destruction. It's because of little ones like those two. If you really want a new life, you'll need to work for it here, because we're struggling too. Maybe together we can create a new chance for them."

DANIEL YOCOM (Genre Writers, Infinite Monkeys) does geeky things at night because his day job won't let him. This dates back to the 1960s through games, books, movies, and stranger things better shared in small groups. He's written hundreds of articles about these topics for his own blog, other websites, and magazines after extensive research along with short stories. His research includes attending conventions, sharing on panels and presentations, and road-tripping with his wife. Join him at guildmastergaming.blogspot.com.

Rebirth

Blithe Anderson

Yesterday Momma told me to pack my bags 'cause we're going to see Grandpa in Elko. She doesn't realize I already have a bag packed. Got a duffel bag under my bed next to the stack of report cards I've been saving. We're supposed to get those report cards signed by our parents, but I told the art teacher, Ms. Jones, that Momma died last fall so no one bugs me about that, anyway. The duffel bag's got enough candy bars for a few days of eating and then my favorite sweater, Stripes, and some jeans. I don't like that Stripes is dedicated to my escape plan, 'cause I never get to wear it anymore. But I figure if I finally get up the guts to run away, I'll wanna take that with me.

"LILY!" That's Momma.

"What, Ma?"

"You better pack up now. We have a long drive and I gotta make a stop at the pharmacy."

When Momma says pharmacy, she really means her drug-dealer's trailer. That man, Steve, has never worn nothin' pure-white like a lab coat in his life. When she makes a stop there, she takes at least an hour getting her prescriptions. Then she floats out of that trailer with a blessing from a dark angel—all calm but she's not really there. I don't know which Momma I prefer, the dope-sick momma or the blessed one.

You're probably wondering where a fourteen-year-old girl like me is fixin' to escape to with a duffel bag full of candy. Well, I'll tell you. I don't know. I just know I have to get out of this place. When I picture leaving, I have a hard time imagining anything past the shutting of the screen door and walking away from this shithole neighborhood.

Last fall, Ma overdosed for the third time. That's when I decided I had to get outta here for good. When I told Ms. Jones Momma died, I didn't lie. She really did die, and then she came back to life when I stuck the Narcan up her nose. I watched that woman get reborn three times, and she never did a thing with those extra chances. The dark angels keep calling her back. I wonder what they tell her when she's dead.

After that, I knew I needed to get reborn, too. Use the chances she wasted. I want to be someone like those influencers on Instagram. Travel the world looking beautiful and feeling beautiful. Every day would be a fresh start and no Momma to speak of.

"LILLAAAYY! Let's GO! Doc's waitin'."

Doc is Steve.

"I'm coming! Just let me get my shoes on. You want me going to Elko without shoes?"

"I don't give a fuck what you do, Lily. I'll be in the car." She grabs her fake Louis Vuitton bag and slams the screen door. It bounces back open and creaks like it always does.

When Ma goes to Steve's, she makes me come with her so I can drive her home, 'cause she can't do shit when she gets well. Plus, she doesn't like staying around Steve when she's high. I think he touches her when she's nodding off, but she won't admit it. That's just what I think.

Our car is twelve years older than I am. It's a 1994

Plymouth Colt that Mom's boyfriend bought her back in the day. Mom used to pick men that would take care of her, but now she's too old, and men don't want to take care of a middle-aged junkie. I don't blame them. I don't like taking care of her, either. On the passenger seat of the car is half a pack of Pyramids. I sit down real lightly on top of them, hoping Momma won't notice they're there so I can take em'.

It's January but it's eighty degrees outside. Killeen doesn't cool down much but it's hotter than it should be this time of year. The Colt's A/C has been out since I was nine, and I'm not looking forward to this long-ass drive to Elko. I'm so sick of driving across the country to get money. Grandpa makes Momma come to his house if she wants cash, so we make the trip every few months to get by.

She pulls out of the skinny driveway and I hear the chimes that hang from our porch. I want this to be the last time I hear them. I want this to be the last time I look at that nasty green carpet leading up to the front door. Last time I see Steve's fucking face. Last time I worry about Momma dying and it being my fault 'cause I'm at school or the grocery store and I can't watch over her.

Every time we get to Steve's, she pulls the sun visor down and looks in the mirror while she puts on bright red lipstick. I don't know why she even tries.

"Okay, baby. I'll be just a minute. You make sure it's on that station I like when I get back. Then it's you and me and the open road."

She's so much sweeter when she's about to pick up. I fucking hate it.

"Tell Steve to eat shit."

"Sure, baby. Whatever you like."

Her eyes are foggy and it's like she's high already.

Fiddling with the radio, I skip her favorite channel but I

land on that Incubus song she likes. I like it too, but I pretend I don't. "Drive," I think it's called.

I light one of the Pyramids and start singing along.

I don't really know what takes over me, but I move to the driver's seat and start the car. I check to see if Ma or Steve hear it start, but no one comes lookin' out any windows. I back out as fast as I can without running into the neighbor's Honda and just drive off.

I don't even look back.

BLITHE ANDERSON (Salt City Genre Writers) writes creative nonfiction, poetry and has begun to dabble in fiction. She has recently been published in Salt Lake City Weekly. In addition, several of her pieces have been curated by the editors of Medium.com, where she's grown a wide audience of readers. Check out more of her writing at medium.com/@blitheanderson.

Give and Take

John M. Olsen

Nobody ever came out of the mines once the king sentenced them to the underground cavern. Worse yet, the labor of the prisoners made it harder to escape as they dug the floor of the cavern deeper over time while searching for leftover bits of magic from the ancient ley-line path.

I examined the fresh rockfall in an alcove off the main cavern. It looked almost like it had fallen on its own, and would pass all but the closest of inspections. Asoka was now free. That's all that mattered. She wouldn't spend another day digging in the mines.

Voices called as miners approached from several directions, summoned by the collapse I'd caused. The first to arrive stopped when they saw me sitting at the edge of the debris field. The rock dust still settled around me, filling my nose with the familiar scent of rubble.

Their whispers carried to me in the dim blue glow of the lightstones about their necks. *Tonglen's lost another partner? He pushed too hard again and collapsed the wall. Why does he do it? Doesn't he care?* Then the one that hurt the most. *Is he murdering them to steal their magic chips?*

I slumped, letting their criticisms wash over me. Soon, they returned to their labors at small pits scattered across the base of the dome. Only one, a wiry young man just out of his teen years, stayed.

"What do you want, Osho?"

"They told me I have to be your new partner. Said I was the runt and would have to fight if I want a better assignment. Didn't feel like losing another fight."

Truth be told, I preferred small partners, but couldn't tell anyone why. Asoka only found out why when it was too late to do anything about it. If I proceeded too fast, it would draw too much attention. If I used too much magic, the guards would notice.

"Well then, let's get to it. I saw a few sparkles in the new collapse." I fetched my tools. Asoka's tools were buried in the collapse, but I knew right where to dig to find them.

Osho climbed his way over the jagged rock, holding his lightstone out to search for the telltale sparks of light given off by the small magical chips.

"Hey, you're right. Got a blink of light over here." He settled in to free the glowing bit from the rock that held it.

"I'll fill my tarp with the overburden and run it to the lift while you break that chip free." It was the least I could do, letting my new partner work on the valuable chips of solid magic while I did the heavy labor. I'd hauled rock for years, and could out-haul all but the hardiest of the miners. I always met—and occasionally exceeded—my quota on both the over-burden and magic chips every day.

The lift we used to remove rock from the pit would have been impossible to run if not for the magic they pumped into it from above. Wizards melted and molded the chips, creating fantastic tools. The lift hauled rock three times each day with the magic chips sorted into boxes according to who dug them.

It came back down with our meager meal rations. No chips, no food.

The chips had uses in the mine as well, even though it was forbidden, and I was the only one I'd ever seen use magic in the pit. The little chips could lift boulders if you knew the right incantation, but the bright light given off by the effort could betray me.

I emptied rocks from my tarp onto the lift. One of the earlier whisperers grew bold. "Are you going to ride up the lift today, Tonglen?"

I shook my head. "You get to suffer through my continued presence." A miner had tried to sneak up the lift a half year past and now his lifeless skull kept watch from where it was fastened to the lift.

Back at the collapse, Osho held three chips in the palm of his hand. A few more, and they would be as bright as his lightstone.

"You do fast work."

"They say I'm lucky. Not like you." He tucked his temporary wealth into a pouch, out of sight. "How many partners have you...lost?"

The implication that I'd killed another partner hung in the air, unspoken. "Six. But you already knew that. Everyone knows. I've heard what everyone says about me. Go ahead. Ask. I know you're curious."

"They say you have a whole pile of chips saved somewhere. That you plan to buy your way out somehow."

I shook my head. "Sorry, I have no pile of treasure. The guards wouldn't accept such a bribe, anyway. They'd end up down here to mine with us." I had no need to lie, which was a relief. I might find twice the chips of anyone else, but I'd used my entire stash mere hours before the rockfall.

Osho climbed over to the wall and tapped his hammer on a

tall column. The stone gave off a strange ringing sound that ran up the wall.

"Stop! Don't hammer there. That old channel is under pressure." I peered upward along the seams and flow of stone, and the old ley-line paths. Sure enough, that one ran up the whole side of the dome as a main support. It might be a good source of chips, but it could also bring the whole dome down. Everyone left the main arch supports alone when they became exposed.

"Fine. I'll go back to the rubble. Probably more chips there anyway."

Had the boy been testing me to see if I knew how to detect the structural supports? Now he would be even more suspicious. It was time to let Osho feel like he had some control.

"Once we clear out the easy chips here, where would you like to try next? One of the pits? Maybe one of the tunnels running out from the dome? Where have you had the best luck?"

"You're one to talk about luck." He banged at a rock until it split along a seam, revealing another chip to break free. "The pits are safe."

I shook my head. "There's nothing safe here. There's only making your quota or not. But if you want to try a pit, we'll do that next." The pits took fewer lives, it was true. But it was harder to make the chip quota.

I'd forgotten how simple the open pit work could be. Break up the rocks. Carry them to the lift. Save the occasional chips and send up the quota. The secret stash of magic chips hidden away inside my rolled cloth belt grew slowly, but I had to bide my time and win over Osho.

The wiry boy tapped at a tall boulder on the side of our

small pit as I fought to free a chip from its surrounding stone. With a sudden cry, Osho fell back as a pillar of stone broke loose and tipped onto him. The stone was tall and skinny, but outweighed him and forced him to the ground.

I stumbled over the rocks and couldn't reach him before the rock landed with a thud, pinning Osho under its bulk. "Hold on, kid. I've got this." I dropped my hammer and grabbed my big prybar and hunted for leverage that wouldn't crush him. It was no good. Leverage required a good fulcrum, and there was none.

"Break it," Osho gasped from under the stone. "Move the pieces."

"Right. And let the top half smash your head when it falls?" I looked around and saw nobody. One of the advantages to working in a small pit on the edge of the main floor.

There, in the exposed face of the rock pinning the boy, sat two magic chips. It would be enough. I grabbed my tarp and spread it over the stone and climbed underneath. "Close your eyes, Osho. Close them tight."

"Don't kill me, Tonglen."

"I'm saving you. Now shut up and close your eyes."

His breath strained to get the words out. "Fine."

Incantations for simple magic were impossible to forget once learned and used. Images flowed into my mind as I placed my fingers onto the visible chips. The stone lifted, and the world underneath the tarp lit up. With the stone levitating, I pushed it to the side as the two chips vanished. The stone crashed to the ground with charred spots where the chips had been.

Afterimages glowed in my eyes. My sight would return, but it would take a few minutes. I rolled the tarp and set it aside. "Are you hurt?"

Osho grunted. "Arm got hit hard." The young man winced and cradled his right arm with his left hand.

I felt up and down his arm. The bones held, but could have been cracked. "You're going to be working one-handed for a while. I'll help with your quota if I have to."

Osho sat, rubbing his arm and staring at me. "There are rumors you're a wizard. Explains a lot." After a long pause, he added, "Thank you."

"I'd hate to lose another partner so soon. Now, let's hope the guards weren't watching, or they'll come down and have words with me." I held out a hand and pulled Osho to his feet by his good hand. "Sorry, but I think I drained all the chips out of your block of stone." Luckily, I hadn't had to draw upon my meager surplus.

Osho fingered the blackened holes in the stone. "We should break this up so they can't tell what you did."

Friendship could grow from such small beginnings. My plan required his trust.

We broke the large rock into pieces. After a long silence, Osho spoke. "Really, why'd you do that?"

"There's a religious group where I was born that believes in transforming pain into aid. Accept the pain of others into yourself, then share emotional and physical aid with others outside yourself. It's a form of meditation. In with the bad, change it, and out with the good."

"You studied under them?" Osho asked.

"I left them when I was still young and foolish, and couldn't see the value in giving up my own time and wealth for others. What benefit is there to giving things away? I succumbed to temptations and learned to gain power at the expense of others. Add the power of wizardry into the mix, and I ruined my life. Before long, I ended up in the king's prison for insulting the wrong person. Then I said something rude about a guard's parentage and got sent here. Finally, I learned that I'd always had the answer I needed."

It had been ages since I'd described the path my life had

taken, and how I'd gained self-control through the teachings of my youth. Finding peace through serving others had put me on the right path after a life of mistakes.

"You're not like they say."

"I was. Believe me, everything they say about me used to be true. I wasted a lot of time taking what I thought would make me happy when I should have worked to make others happy. Now, I'm afraid I'll have to swear you to secrecy. I can't have them finding out I'm actually nice." I winked. "Let's put that arm in a sling and get back to work."

There were rumors that the guards squeezed the time between lifts to get more magic chips from the miners. I was the only one in the pit who had proof, and I couldn't share it. Even so, everyone in the pit counted days by the meals they ate. Even if the count was wrong, all the prisoners agreed on the count.

Days didn't matter as much as the magic chips I gathered through hard work with Osho. Soon he set aside the sling, but still favored the arm. The young man asked a never-ending stream of questions about magic, how the incantations worked, and what they could do. "How high can you lift something?" Osho poked a thumb at the ceiling.

"That takes too much magic. Besides, the guards that watch the lift are always there." I made a falling gesture with my hand, landing on a stone with a slap. I would have liked to wait a little longer, but the boy's questions probed deeper each day. Soon, others might overhear. Between us, we had enough magic saved up. "What do you say we take a look a little farther out? I know a tunnel I think you'll like."

The nervous look on Osho's face showed I hadn't won him over yet. Doubts remained, although he'd never been brave enough to ask how the other partners had been lost. "Are you sure that's a good idea?" He probably didn't want his stash stolen.

"Don't worry. We can come back to the pits if you don't like it. Let's leave right after dinner."

Sitting near the lift with a bowl of gruel, Osho watched me with a wrinkled brow, as if trying to read the future on my face. "You have to tell me. What's in the tunnel?"

"Not here. No questions." I silenced my partner with an abrupt wave of the hand. It could ruin everything if others heard, or even if they suspected today was the day. Cutting off my partner like that would only enhance my reputation among those who already feared or hated me. I swallowed the last of the tasteless food and said, "Let's go. We have work to do."

We picked up our meager mining tools, and I led my young partner through a series of pits and chipped out arches ending at the edge of the dome. There, I used my pick to clear a low entrance just big enough to scoot through on my belly. "You first, Osho. I'm right behind you. It opens up after the third bend."

He nodded after a moment and crawled into the hole.

The day I discovered the tunnel had been a disaster and a triumph. The entrance had collapsed with both me and my digging partner inside. Rather than dig our way out immediately, we had hoped to find an easier path back, but the tunnel continued farther away from the main dome.

After a time, we had stepped out of the tunnel into a smooth-walled shaft where we gawked, looking upward. A small side-shaft near the top glowed not with the light of magic, but with sunlight. Sunlight and freedom.

I watched my partner's face as he entered the same shaft and looked upward to the light, like all my partners had.

"I have a story to tell you, Osho. My first partner and I discovered this shaft by accident. There's no telling what magical or natural forces created it, but that glow up there is the light of glorious sunshine. When we first found this spot, we waited to be sure, watching that opening grow dark when night overtook the outside world. It was glorious, but we were down here, and the tunnel was up there."

"You used magic."

I nodded. "Yes. He insisted that I use up all our magic chips to lift him. I made him promise to go for help. He never came back, but at least he was free. I have no idea if he made it to safety or if he was discovered and killed. There's no way to know. I've told this story to every partner since, and they've all chosen to take the same risk. A chance at freedom is better than a guaranteed death in the mine. What do you say?"

"None of them ever came back?"

"None. If you make it to safety, all I ask is that you come back and leave a rope. I've asked each partner, but they've never come back. Now you have to choose."

"You going to kill me if I say no?"

I laughed. "You're thinking of the image the other prisoners have of me. If you say no, we go back and you never speak of it again. I bribe someone to trade partners, then stage an accident to claim they died and their body is lost, just like the others."

"You know, some say you eat them."

"It figures. What's your choice?"

Osho shuffled and gazed upward. "Why don't you lift yourself and get out?"

"I can't. Maybe I could with a different incantation, but the one I have won't work that way." The delays and questions were a torture to endure. "Can you decide already? I want to get back to the dome and fake your death."

Osho laughed and handed over his chips. "Do it."

Handing one chip back, I said, "This will be worth several days of food out there. Maybe even weeks. I can lift you with the rest of our chips." I'd been counting, estimating how many chips Osho had saved. Without the last chip, it would work. Barely.

"Leave your tools. They're too heavy. Now hold still and cover your eyes with your hands. Just closing them isn't always good enough."

With a handful of chips, the simple incantation set off a blinding light as Osho rose. An occasional squinting glance up was all I could afford as my partner rose to the ledge. "Quickly! Pull yourself into the tunnel. The chips are almost gone."

The light died, and there was no crash of a body hitting the floor. Osho had made it.

"Holy starlight! There's a rope hidden up here. Climb up and join me." A knotted rope snaked out over the lip and dangled along the wall with a bit of extra rope dragging on the floor. "Already tied off at one end, too."

With a sense of shock flowing through me from head to toe, I said, "She came back for us. Asoka made it out and came back." After so many questions, now I knew. The partners he'd rescued weren't tracked down and killed. It was true freedom that beckoned, and not just a chance to be free of the cave for a day until hunted down and killed by guards. Visions of sunlight and fresh breezes filled me. The scent of leaves and grass rose up from old memories. Then my heart ached for a different reason. "I can't go. What about the others? Can we doom them to stay while we flee?"

Osho sat on the lip of the drop off and dangled his feet next to the rope. "Take what you can. You don't owe any of them a thing. Most of them don't even like you. Don't trust you, either."

"You should leave. I'll go back to convince them." I turned to the cave and shouldered his tools beside mine, preparing for the return trip. The rope meant I was no longer limited to one rescue every few weeks or months. Everyone could get out now.

From above, Osho cursed. "Hold up. You'll never convince them without me." He shimmied down the rope, still favoring his injured arm, then pulled out a small blade to chop off the end that dragged on the cave floor. He sawed at it until the length came free in his hand. "Our proof."

The trip back passed much faster than normal, with no thoughts of having to lie to my fellow prisoners. This time, I could tell the truth. I would take in all their sorrows and give them the joy of a new chance at life as my continued penance. Peace filled my heart like never before, but something nagged at me. Something that didn't quite feel right, like I'd forgotten to lace my sandals and was about to trip on the cords.

We approached the lift as the workers loaded it for the day's last trip.

Osho waved me off and approached people as they arrived, talking—and quietly arguing—with them. I stayed back, letting the boy have his way to speak with them first. Against all odds, they stayed rather than heading to their meager bedrolls to sleep. Soon, over a hundred miners sat and waited as they conversed and glanced my way.

The boy had worked a miracle getting them to stay by showing them the end of the rope, something nobody in the mine should own.

Before I could stand to address them, Osho stood and waved at me to stay sitting. "Going to be a long night, here. Remember what I said to you. Tonglen knows a way out, and we can all go. Get your things and follow us."

It wasn't much as far as motivational speeches went, and I wondered what the boy had said to them as they arrived. If it worked, none of that mattered. They eyed me, some with fear, some with curiosity. None approached me. They were so used to being told what to do that most accepted Osho's direction without resistance. Many were so tired that they didn't care if freedom called, or if he led them to their doom. One of the more optimistic prisoners said, "That will be quite a surprise when the guards see us all gone like magic."

Guards. I'd forgotten that part, despite giving everyone a story for each of my earlier rescues. The guards would find out we were gone, would search the hills outside, and then kill us.

I nearly called a halt to the procession following Osho, but an idea came to me. Like a new meditation exercise, I would take in their grief and trouble, and give the answer to free them. A final penance.

I hurried along the procession, telling each group, "Be sure we have everyone. Anyone who stays will be killed." They nodded with fear in their eyes. Some went in search of missing miners.

Upon reaching the head of the procession, I pulled Osho forward. "What did you tell them? They act like I'll skin them alive if they disobey."

His guilty expression increased my curiosity. "I don't know what you mean."

As we approached the low entrance to the tunnel, I stopped the first miner behind us. "What did Osho tell you?"

"Why, that you would use your magic to kill anyone who stayed behind, like you told us just now. We've seen those light flashes where you work. We all know you're a wizard."

"I…" My words came back to me, and I realized my warning could be seen as a threat. Osho shrugged apologetically.

The boy had found a way to expand and play upon their fear. If it saved them, so be it. I would play the hand I was dealt. "Osho, I'm going to bring the dome down when you have everyone out." The nearest critical support sat where Osho and I had worked, not far away.

"But you're out of chips."

"I have a pick, a hammer, and a prybar. It will do."

Osho scratched the sparse beard starting on his chin. "You'll die."

"Almost certainly. I'd rather not, but if they think we've escaped, we all die. I'm open to ideas."

"Magic."

I'd used all my chips, and turned the folds of my belt to show it held nothing. "It would take more than I've ever saved to make it work. I'm old. I've had a long run. You know the way."

"Cut the noble sacrifice act, old man. What do you need?"

"A protected passage from the support pillar to the cave entrance, and some chips to keep the tunnel from collapsing on me when the roof comes down." It was like asking for the sun and moon.

"You care about people, but you don't understand them. That's why none of them ever came back until you lucked into having Asoka as a partner. See these people? Watch and learn."

He stood on a boulder and raised his lightstone as he shouted. "The great wizard Tonglen requires two things of you. We need a protected passage from this cave entrance to that pillar over there." Osho waved at the support before digging out his single chip of magic and handing it over with a flourish. "He also needs more magic."

A man spoke up. "I've gone along so far, but I'm not doing anything more for this *great wizard* until he shows he can get us out."

Osho looked from the man to me and back, leaving me to handle the problem. Great help that boy was, losing his silver tongue when it mattered the most.

I sized up a large boulder that sat in almost the right spot, and a flat piece I could wedge between it and the cavern wall as a roof. Maybe Osho had the right approach, giving the people an authority figure to rely on. I stood tall, playing the part of an all-knowing wizard, and hoped the man didn't think back to all the years when I'd groveled and dug in the pit like everyone else. "Give me three chips of magic." I held my hand out to the man who demanded a sign.

"Now look away from the chips, or risk going blind." I wasn't going to use the tarp for this. It had to be showy.

The chips glowed like the sun, and the boulder rolled closer to the wall as I pushed it. Then the cap for the tunnel section lifted. Just before settling into place, the chips ran out, and the rock dropped with a bang that echoed through the chamber.

My vision bore spots, but temporary blindness didn't block out the sound of alarms from the ceiling. I'd made a critical error. They'd seen. "We have to hurry. There's no time to build the safe path. The guards will be upon us soon."

The alarms invigorated the miners. I set my tarp out to collect their chips of magic as they entered the tunnel. "Keep one chip. Now go as fast as you can."

Osho knew all the best hiding spots for the magic chips, and he shook down the prisoners as they passed and crawled into the narrow tunnel. He must have been a great thief before coming to the mine.

Now Osho would have to lead them to safety if I didn't make it. "Everyone will need to travel as far away from here as they can. Make them scatter."

"But you're coming with us. That's what the chips are for, right?"

"I've never done anything this big. That's a lot of lifting. Don't wait too long for me." After patting him on the back, I sent him to the narrow cave entrance.

The pile of chips felt warm to the touch as I scooped them into my hands. I'd never seen so many in one place.

Across the cavern, I heard the platform land with a

grinding thud. The guards formed up and worked their way across the rough floor, lamps held high. I couldn't let them report on the abandoned camp.

Throwing caution to the wind, I located the biggest free boulder in the area. I pinched my eyes shut as hard as I could. Magic flowed as the chips softened and clumped together in a ball. I sensed the boulder through the magic as it lifted. I hurtled it toward the wall. Stone hit stone with a colossal crash, and rock splinters peppered my skin.

Then nothing. I peeked through my squinting eyes. The rock pillar held with the boulder wedged into it. Closing my eyes again, I used all but a tiny bit of the magic to twist the stone and pull it free. Great slabs fell from the wall, then tumbled from higher reaches until the roof itself dropped great sheets of stone. Sunlight streamed through cracks into the collapsing pit for the first time ever.

I stood, mesmerized by the image of sunlight on stone as rock fell around me until a hand grabbed my shoulder and pulled me toward our now-blocked escape tunnel. I used the last of my pooled magic to push the debris clear, and to push away approaching rocks as we scurried through. The earth shook as the remaining roof collapsed behind us in a thunderous roar. The earth continued to groan and shake as we followed the narrow tunnel.

Emerging at the shaft to freedom, I turned to thank Osho for coming back for me, but instead saw the man who had insisted on seeing my magic. He pointed me to the rope and followed me up to freedom. "You were right, Tonglen. Thank you."

Outside, we stood on the mountain and watched billowing clouds of dust rise from a giant steep-walled pit a short distance below us. In the sunshine, I realized I hadn't saved them to atone for the sins of my youth. I'd given them freedom because I cared. Their lives were now their own, and I could return to the home and teachings of my childhood. It remained to be seen whether I could teach the next generation, or if they would have to learn the path the hard way like I had.

JOHN M. OLSEN (Herriman Chapter) edits and writes speculative fiction across multiple genres, and loves stories about ordinary people stepping up to do extraordinary things. He hopes to entertain and inspire others with his award-winning stories as he passes his passion on to the next generation of avid readers.

He loves to create and fix things, whether editing or writing novels or short stories or working in his secret lair equipped with dangerous power tools. In all cases, he applies engineering principles and processes to the task at hand, often in unpredictable ways.

You can find his Riland Throne fantasy trilogy (starting with *Crystal King*) on Amazon along with dozens of his short stories.

He lives in Utah with his lovely wife and a variable number of mostly grown children and a constantly changing subset of extended family.

Check out his ramblings on his blog at johnmolsen.blogspot.com.

The Liberty of Conflict

Danielle Harward

Holland's leg was hurting. I could tell by the way he leaned against his cane to keep the weight off. But he had been in worse pain, and he wasn't about to slow down now.

At the Smithsonian's National Museum of American History, we rounded the corner to the viewing glass with the Star-Spangled Banner flag behind it. I noted his breath catch.

I couldn't blame him; mine did too.

The 34-foot-long ripped and burned flag which inspired our nation's anthem was stunning. And if I felt that way about it, I could only imagine how he felt.

Holland, my grandfather, had fought in Vietnam and had been awarded a purple heart for his bravery. He took a bullet in the leg during his last mission. His brothers in arms did what they could for him in the field, but by the time the mission was complete, the bullet in his leg had spread an infection. The field medics did all they could. They were able to give him his life, but not the full function of his leg. So, he had come back to my mother (who was a teenager at the time) and his wife with a new medal, a cane, and a smoking habit to manage the pain.

He put an arm around my slim shoulders and squeezed. I was tall, but still small for a man of our family. Large shoulders and towering height seemed to skip over me at birth. My grandfather, whose back was crooked from old age, stood at six feet three inches. Two inches taller than me.

"Jason, this was a good idea," he murmured.

He squeezed my shoulder again, taking one last longing look at the flag which had inspired so many, before moving along.

Holland had been diagnosed with terminal lung cancer, and I wanted these memories in Washington, D.C. with him. Selfish perhaps, but he had taught me to go after what I wanted with no regrets, so I did. He and I didn't always see eye to eye, making our relationship difficult at times, but I was his favorite grandchild, and he was my favorite grandfather. Our differences hadn't separated us.

The National Archives were next, and it was one of the places I was most excited about seeing. Luckily, it was only a short walk away. I slowed my pace as I walked, and Holland raised an eyebrow my way.

"You fading on me kid?"

"I think you could use a break."

He pointed a well wrinkled finger at the long line wrapping around the National Archives. "I think I'll have plenty of time to sit around."

I smirked and matched his pace. He glared at those who walked too close to him on the sidewalk. Even with a crooked back my grandfather kept his head as high as possible. The military uniform he wore added to his intimidation factor.

Holland's lip curled as a group of young men exited from the archives with loud whoops as they jostled each other. Before we took our place in line, he tapped a cigarette out of its box and stuffed it between his lips as he mumbled, "People like them shouldn't even be allowed into a place like this."

I rolled my eyes and leaned against a bench as he lit up and pulled in a heavy drag, eyeing the line with suspicion. Probably scoping out any other potential hooligans.

The group of young men headed down the walk and turned our way. They shouted and pushed each other. I could easily hear them above the murmur of the crowd. All were about my age, bachelors by the looks of it, like me. Though Holland had always given me hell about not finding someone to settle down with, rambling on about how he and everyone he knows was married by the age of twenty, I hadn't yet found the right person. And between the complexities of online dating and struggling to be financially secure, I doubted I'd find someone soon.

Holland exhaled in annoyance as the group neared us.

I noted the diversity of the group as they weaved through the crowd. Between the six of them, there were at least four races. Two of the men held each other's hands as the others talked loudly around them. Not all of them were single then.

As they began to pass, Holland stepped on his cigarette.

They were almost clear of us when one of them turned, looking my grandfather up and down. "Hey man," he called. "Are you a veteran?"

I thought Holland might spit on him by the way his eyes shot daggers at the young man, but instead he nodded. Once.

The young man broke away from the group. I pegged him as Indian, but I didn't like to assume. He stopped in front of us and threw up his hand in a high five gesture. "That's awesome, man!"

His hand stayed suspended there, waiting for my grandfather to react. It was kind of him to acknowledge us, but I knew by the look on Holland's face that he hadn't done so the 'right' way. Still, he waited, patiently smiling.

After several beats of awkward silence Holland gave him

an answer. "You and your . . , group . . . are too loud. Have some respect."

The young man frowned, pulling his hand back. He glanced at me and I mouthed "sorry" to the poor guy. He shrugged and turned to catch up with his friends.

Holland watched him go with a heavy stare. After a long moment he moved forward again, heading for the end of the National Archives line, his cigarette finished.

"You see that, Jason? Millennials! They don't even know how to say hello."

I glanced at the group walking away again. The young man who Holland had refused to high five looked unphased.

"He was trying to thank you for your service," I pointed out.

"Then he can shake my hand like a man."

"What does it matter how he does it?"

We all moved forward a few steps as the line advanced.

"Someday I hope you understand that it's lazy not to offer a man your hand when speaking with him."

I had heard that plenty of times before. And not just from Holland. *Lazy* was thrown around so much it seemed like it was practically the definition of a millennial. People usually define someone else as *lazy* when they don't do the same action as everyone else. I didn't like the word, but I chose to change the subject instead.

"What are you most excited to see here?"

My grandfather was a brave man, but he was also self-absorbed. I loved him and his faults, but I also knew I could get him talking about anything else if I asked a question about himself. He would readily answer it.

Our topics of discussion ranged as we waited in line surrounded by fifty or so strangers. It was always easy to talk to Holland. He had the best stories and could carry a conversation for hours. Yes, the topic usually ended up on him eventually, but I didn't mind. It took me back to sitting by the fire with him and listening to his stories. He had taught me about so many of my personal heroes, it only made sense he was one of them. He had been more of a dreamer then. I remember when he wasn't so easy to anger and his criticisms weren't always so harsh. However, in recent years as his health and movement declined, he became angrier. My father told me he was angry at the world. But I knew from years of therapy that anger stems from somewhere deep inside.

When we got to the door, the receptionist who traded our money for tickets shook my grandfather's hand and thanked him for his service warmly.

His mood instantly brightened.

"You see," he told me as we headed in, "she understands how to greet a veteran."

I glanced back at her. She was older than me - I pegged her in her early thirties.

"You know, she's also a millennial."

"Posh! That's doubtful. A bunch of disconnected, coddled, entitled brats they are."

Sometimes, I wondered if he realized I'm in the "damned millennial" generation he seemed to hate. I knew I was right, but I pushed a different way.

"Everyone I know is respectful to their elders. Even that guy was being respectful, in his own way."

"Someone needs to teach him some decorum then."

"Why can't it be both ways?"

Holland limped along, leaving me behind to say he was done with the conversation.

I debated bringing up the fact that millennials are often the object of media hyperventilation. But it was a hard topic to discuss with someone who couldn't do much. He often spent most of his day reading and listening to the news, and I knew what those articles said. They claimed we were ruining several industries like cable TV, casual chain restaurants, and home-ownership. Industries which had stood at the pinnacle of my parents' and grandparents' generations.

But he had moved on, so I did too.

When we got to the Constitution, Holland and I both looked it over with wonder.

"Our founding fathers were wise beyond their years," Holland murmured.

I nodded. "I've always loved that they started the constitution with, 'We the people . . . . .' They wanted to include everyone in these rights."

Holland grinned at me. His eyes crinkled with warmth.

As we continued, we enjoyed the rest of the archives in mutual silence, taking in the murals around us. It wasn't until we made it to the gift shop that Holland spoke.

"I'll meet you outside," he said as I started to drift into the gift shop.

He wasn't one for material things, but that was code for needing a smoke, and I recognized it quick enough. I nodded to him as he limped away and I began perusing. It wasn't long until I landed on a small book titled *"The Founding Fathers: Quotes, Quips, and Speeches"* by Gordon Leidner. Opening it up to the first page, I read the following:

"The founders believed God had destined America to be a separate country, a beacon of liberty, and a model of better government for future generations."

Those words rang through me. How right Gordon was. They were liberating—our founding fathers—and I loved learning about them. Holland would probably enjoy it as well. I purchased the book and headed out, excited to show him.

He stood on the steps. A cigarette poked from his lips as he scowled at the citizens who moved past him.

"We used to be the greatest nation on earth," he grumbled

as I approached. I frowned up at him, pivoting to stay downwind from his smoke.

"What changed?" I asked.

"It's millennials," he grumbled. "They are ruining the country."

I tucked the book back into its gift shop bag and braced myself for an argument. It would be one of many, and definitely not our last.

"Why?"

Holland's sharp eyes cut into me as he got a drag from his cigarette. He was the type of man who didn't like to be contradicted. To him, anything but an agreement was a contradiction, and I had contradicted him too many times today. I waited, letting the silence fall between us like heavy rocks. Perhaps he wouldn't answer me.

His lip curled with his response. "They don't know what hard work is. Freedom was won for them by the blood of true Americans, and what are they doing with it? Playing around on their phones and posting tweets."

Such a bold, dramatic statement. He glanced toward a group of teenagers just off a field trip bus who were taking selfies and likely posting them on various social media accounts. Now, I knew where his bad mood had come from. It was an effort not to remind him that the millennial generation was much older than these school kids. It seemed that anyone who was younger than my grandfather and did something to annoy him was a millennial these days.

Perhaps I should have left it. This was a standard gripe. Something I was used to. I typically tuned it out and continued on with my day. But he kept bringing this up, and it was starting to put a hamper on our vacation. Why couldn't he just enjoy this time with me?

I thought he'd love coming here. When I was a young boy, he taught me about the formation of our government. We'd have long conversations as we discussed political parties. He was the reason I wanted to come in the first place. I thought we would be able to share this vacation together and explore our capitol with wonder.

"Millennials understand freedom–"

"Now, see here. If they understood freedom, they wouldn't be wasting it. Good Americans bled for the rights they take advantage of today."

I hated being interrupted. Funny enough, it was something I had picked up from my grandfather. He hated being interrupted too, yet loved to interrupt. I resisted the urge to cough as his exhale of smoke wafted closer to my face.

"How are they wasting it if they push for the freedom of others?"

His eyes darkened. I had opposed him again. Practically an assault on his front. He was worried about me, believed college had made me too liberal. Of course, to him one was liberal if they disagreed with hard conservative views in any way.

His curled lip turned into a snarl as he pulled his stub of a cigarette from his mouth and tapped it on an ashtray trash can combo. The reek of the trash inside mixed with his smoke.

"Don't you disagree with me, boy," he murmured much like a gun slinger just before the draw. "I've been on this earth for far longer than you."

No one disagrees with my grandfather, and I was no stranger as to why. But it was important to note that the collage Holland worried about also gave me the ability to understand when he was wrong. Something the rest of my family usually assumed but couldn't confirm.

"Why do you think they don't understand freedom?" I pushed as he looked away from me. He wanted me to stop talking.

"Why do you think they do?"

I was prepared for that avoidance tactic. He didn't have examples.

"Because they find the freedom of others so important— like gay marriage, freedom of speech, and equality. Isn't that what freedom truly is? Freeing others?"

"Don't quote that Toni Morrison bull," Holland snapped. "All you listed was the Democratic crap pushed in the media."

Democratic crap. This wasn't a surprise either, but it was enough to make my blood boil. I wasn't even a Democrat–I was a Libertarian. Not that he had ever asked.

"You think millennials are ruining things? Let's talk about the 19 trillion in government debt your generation left behind for us. Or the decline in federal budgeting for education. Or maybe, let's talk about how endangered our planet has become due to climate change. Who do you think is the cause of that?"

If he wanted to talk about the faults of a generation, maybe we should have started with his own.

"Please," Holland grunted. "You millennials are too soft. It's made you lazy and whiny. Always complaining that the world we gave you isn't enough because you are too focused on the fantasy in your phones."

So, he did think of me as a millennial. Somehow that hurt worse.

People stared at us now. I didn't care, and neither did my grandfather.

"You know social media activism is a thing, right? There are people making serious changes in the world from their phones."

Holland scoffed. "Making a change in the world doesn't come from sitting on the couch and staring at the screen. It comes with hard work, long hours, and battle wounds."

I frowned. Of course he would target relaxing. God forbid I lay on the couch for a moment.

"Oh yes, and all that hard work will get us what? Social

Security and Medicare won't be able to pay us back by the time we retire. Now we have to rely on ourselves to have enough money once we are done working. And how can we do that when there are job shortages? And the jobs that are available require five years of experience for an entry level position."

His lips arched back, revealing yellowed teeth, "Do you think the founding fathers built this country so millennials could destroy it with their wasteful, greedy, and entitled attitudes? Do you think I watched decent American men die so you could dick around on your phone?"

My gut twisted, but he had gotten me started, and I couldn't seem to stop. The words poured out of me before I could stop them. I looked pointedly at the cigarettes as he reached for another.

"Do you think the founding fathers built this country, so you could destroy it and yourself with your cigarette smoke as you pass judgment? Or do you think they built it so others could also be free? Plenty of people around you are advancing freedom. Just because it doesn't look like the freedom you understand doesn't mean it's not freedom! If you understood that maybe others in our family could stand to be around you for more than an hour."

Holland clamped his lips shut, and we were silent for some time. My rage slowly ebbed into something smaller, something that made me queasy. I saw a wetness in his eyes that I had only seen once before.

"I can't believe you were raised to say such hurtful things, Jason," he hissed. "If that's how your mother has taught you to speak to an elder, I truly have failed."

Ah. The guilt trip. A classic which had always hurt my mother and had quickly ended arguments between them. Luckily, it didn't work on me, because I saw how he was trying to strike back. The gunslinger had taken his shot.

Even though I saw through it, the words did sting. Not because of what he had said, but because he had resorted to manipulating me, his grandson, to win an argument.

But why wouldn't he? Didn't I just do the same?

Now, it was my turn to be silent as I looked over the crowd bustling past. They hurried by so as not to draw our anger. Perhaps I had picked up more than a hatred of being interrupted from Holland.

I knew I didn't have much time with him left.

I exhaled deeply, trying to push my anger away with the air leaving my body.

"Can I show you something?" I asked quietly.

He seemed to be done smoking, for now. Maybe feeling like he had won had kicked his need for the moment. He was cautious though. I could tell he was trying to figure out if I was trying to gain the upper hand or not, but he gave me a quick nod.

I pulled out a picture of him when he was young. I always kept it in my wallet. It was a well worn photo which my grandmother had passed down to me when she died. It showed her and my grandfather, holding each other in front of a beautiful valley.

Holland softened when he saw the picture, his gaze taking in every detail.

"When I was little, it was you who taught me about freedom. Your stories filled me with so much wonder. When I got older, the stories may have changed, but the values behind them never did. You made me believe in not only freedom, but in a government and its people. You are the reason I support activism and coexistence with others. I've always dreamed of coming here with you, because I have you to thank for who I am."

My grandfather took the small worn picture gently in his hands and stroked it with a thumb.

"I know my generation's fight for freedom may not come with bombs and bullets like yours did, but it comes with it's own hardships. And we are trying to do the best we can with what we have."

As I finished, Holland took a last long look at the photo before handing it back to me. He wiped at his eyes and gazed forward. I was silent as I gently tucked one of my most prized possessions back into my wallet.

Then, my grandfather snorted. *Snorted*!

I frowned up at him. The wetness in his eyes was gone, and they were softer as he gazed down at me.

"Hardship?" he asked. "Your generation doesn't know what hardship is."

He headed down the steps, pushing into the crowd on the sidewalk with little care. I followed, easily keeping pace as we headed back to the hotel. I could tell I had broken through his walls. His voice was still pragmatic, but his anger seemed to be gone for the moment.

"Actually, we do. These damned boomers have ruined the country." I said as I nudged him with my elbow.

Holland's lip quirked up as he tapped out another cigarette. He gazed forward as he talked, the smile on his lips apparent as he told about how I was "completely uneducated on the subject". However, the light in his eyes didn't fade as he started on another long-winded rant.

I didn't mind. That was the liberty of conflict after all. Two people could have different points of view, upbringings, beliefs, and political affiliations. They could disagree with each other. But the power of discussing those viewpoints, of opening someone's eyes to a broader understanding than they once knew, even if they opposed it, was a freedom Holland and I both cherished.

And I don't think we would ever disagree on that.

DANIELLE HARWARD (Infinite Monkeys) is a high fantasy author who enjoys spinning tales full of heroes and magic. Her work explores the difficulty of conquering inner conflict and the line between good and villainous themes. She gains her inspiration from frequent Dungeons and Dragons sessions and discussing political and emotional conflicts with her husband and friends. And she has ideas for several series which she has a hard time choosing which to write about first.

As a full-time employee and mother, Danielle finds time to write in the wee hours of the night or at the crack of dawn – depending on how exhausted she is by the end of the day. But juggling writing, family, and work is worth it for her because she has wanted to be a writer since she was eight years old and began reading her first fantasy novel.

She holds an Associates degree in Business Management from Snow College and is a member of The League of Utah Writers. She has published several news articles with *The Chronicle Progress* and a short story through The League of Utah Writers Anthology. And she lives in Utah with her husband, their son, and two dogs who silently cheer her on with snuggles on her feet while she writes.

POETS' BREAKFAST GIVEN FOR WRITERS

PROVO—Carrying out a theme of "all men are poets at heart," Mrs. Olive W. Burt, Salt Lake City, president of the state chapter, League of Western Writers, presented prominent Utah writers at a poets' breakfast here Monday morning to open the third annual writers' round-up at Brigham Young university.

Among poets at the breakfast were Mrs. Ethel Romig Fuller, poetry editor of the Oregonian, Portland, Ore., who declared that a hectic and somewhat leftist style is characterizing modern poetry in keeping with the times. "This is especially noticeable among the younger writers," she said.

Salt Lake Telegram | July 18, 1938

You Are My Freedom

Elizabeth Suggs

They said you would be beautiful, but I didn't expect this. Your breath is warm; your heart is strong. On the rare moments you open your eyes, I see bright green and gold gems. You are an angel put on this earth.

They said your twos would be terrible, but I love every moment, even when you cry, because if I wait long enough, I'll see that smile again.

They said when you became a teenager, you would raise hell, but all I see is independence. I see a child who pushes boundaries, who needs to understand herself before going out into the big, scary world. You are so smart, so beautiful.

They said when you became an adult and lived on your own, I wouldn't be able to bear it. That I would cry and try to coerce you to stay. They said I wouldn't be emotionally mature enough to handle your departure. They said I couldn't love you unless I kept you close, but that can't be further from the truth. I am happier when you're free, even when I don't see you for months. You are my child, my love, my angel. There is nothing so perfect as you, and even on my deathbed, when it's my last goodbye, I'll be happy you're alive without me. I want you to be freer than I ever was.

ELIZABETH SUGGS (Romance Writers, Infinite Monkeys, Salt City Genre Writers) is a writer, an editor, and a leader in the writing community. She obsessively writes each morning, lunch, and evening. When she's not writing, she's leading a group of writers through bi-weekly workshops on feedback and focused writing. She believes these meetings help writers understand themselves in the world and better prepare them for major publishers.

She will be published in three anthologies, two horrors, and this anthology, a podcast, as well as a poetry journal this year. She also helped an author publish his children's book.

She used to be a journalist, so many of her publications are nonfiction hard news and events, but she hopes to break the pattern and publish works of art in fiction and poetry, just like the authors she loves reading.

If you'd like to connect with her, please find her on Twitter @elizabethasuggs or visit www.editingmee.com.

Love's Dawn of Freedom: A Message to the World

Marie Tollstrup

What light is to the eyes-what air is to the lungs-what love is to the heart, liberty is to the soul of man.

Robert Green Ingersoll

Loud and long may freedom peal
from bell-tower steeple.

Liberty simmers in summer love
in '76. Adams, Jefferson,
Franklin, far from their lovers'
arms, smolder with desire
for their women, but Independence
Hall imprisons them

while they sculpt the words
of self-rule. As they take sure aim
at their target freedom. Minds
afire, their sweaty bodies
are trapped, and they chip away
steely arguments against autonomy.
Loud and long may freedom peal
from bell-tower steeple.

Armor-clad Adams, lawyer supreme,
struts onto the battlefield
jousting with delegates, ever aware
of formidable foes like
Pennsylvania's John Dickinson's
position, his staunchest antagonist.

In private moments, Adams
climbs bell-tower steps to write
his Angel Abigail. Their many love
letters stand as living testimony
where Abigail acts as America's
first women's advocate.
Loud and long may freedom peal
from bell-tower steeple.

Dr. Franklin, sage diplomat
to England and France, negotiates
with aplomb a long-distance
love affair with Margaret
Stevenson and Madame Brillon
de Jouy, his ardent devotees.

Ben's sizzling words: *We spawned*
a new nationality; we need
a new nation to ignite glowing
revolution. Confronting James Wilson
in a polled Pennsylvania tally,
Ben scores freedom's unanimous vote.
Loud and long may freedom peal
from bell-tower steeple.

Jefferson, the facile word weaver,
his heart ablaze for wife Martha,
pines for her with a ferocity akin
to his passions of self-determination,
music, and science. Adams and Franklin,
midwives to Jefferson's declaration,

hear the Muse's ringing
timbre: *We hold these truths*
to be self-evident. . . all men
are created equal. Jefferson honors
July 4th, not by birthday, but dying
on freedom's 50th anniversary.
Loud and long may freedom peal
from bell-tower steeple.

Independence in '76 hangs
in the balance despite men of mettle
debating its merits. Staunch leaders
know intuitively all men's
souls thrive under freedom's flag.
Toasting Liberty with amber

drafts of ale, the Founders *mutually*
pledge to each other our Lives,
our Fortunes, our sacred Honor.
Freedom, the Phoenix, rising from
war's ashes, demonstrates to mankind
what arouses men to immortality.
Loud and long may freedom peal
from bell-tower steeple.

MARIE TOLLSTRUP (Heritage Writers Guild) is a former teaching nun in the Chicago area. When she left the order, she continued her teaching career in Long Beach, CA, where she specialized in Creative Writing. She founded, advised, and produced *STYLUS*, a national award winning literary/art magazine at Jordan High School for 23 years. After teaching full-time for 39 years, she retired in 1997 and launched her own writing career. Marie has won numerous awards for her prose and poetry at the national, state, and local levels. Her poetry has been published in *The Southern Quill, Panorama, Utah Sings,* eight consecutive LUW anthologies, and *St. George Magazine.* Currently she is the contest chair for Redrock's National Chaparral Poetry Contest. Feel free to contact Marie on Facebook.

Raven Hair

J.E. Zarnofsky

My hair spills onto the ground as I fall, glistening like raven feathers in the moonlight. I don't try to stand. That path leads to more pain. More anger. He seeks out struggle like a hawk snatches a rabbit. So I lay motionless, dead to the world around me.

I hate myself for hiding in plain sight.

But no matter what I try, this is my only way to survive.

He leaves, kicking mud into my face as he goes, making the final punctuation to his show of power. I breathe easier, but only for a moment. His drunken slurs stay, swirling around me and keeping me on the ground. I can barely keep my head up as I tread in their smothering wake. Everything tries to pour out of me at once. I swallow it, choke on it, and I drown. My body convulses. There is more inside of me than I can hold, but if I burst…

If he comes back…

I close my eyes. The hot sting of tears burns deep canyons into my cheeks, down my neck, as they pour onto the dirt beneath me. They soak the already damp ground. The dark spots fade before my eyes, blending outwards until they disappear.

The crunch of gravel beneath leather boots fractures the surrounding silence as someone nears. A bird croaks at the approach. I dare not open my eyes for fear it is him, again, returning for one final blow. It is better if he thinks me dead. Then I could slip away, never to darken my own door again.

"You'll get run over by a horse cart if you keep lying in the road," Aaron says, pity soaking his words.

I roll and turn away without looking at him. Empty, hollow words sting more than the hand that left its mark across my face. His tender words serve no use.

"Let me help you."

I sit up and ignore his extended hand, brushing the dirt off of my apron. It doesn't clear the filth. Mud smears deeper into the woven fibers. I'll have to spend more time at the river washing it out than if I would have just left it untouched. It will give me a longer escape, more reason to not return to the house.

I push myself off the ground. "You want to help me?" I know there is no point in asking, but I cannot stop myself. The faint light of hope lures me like a moth, too foolish to realize it will be burned, time and time again. "Then help me. Let me go with you to the market, Aaron. You're never gone long and I just want to see…"

He does not directly acknowledge my question, but there's a pause. A catch of his breath. A twitch of the eye. A turn of the lip. He's angry that I've asked. I shouldn't have asked. They will never let me be free. "You can't come with me."

"Please, you will not even know that I'm there. I can spare a few hours. He is drunk. He won't even know." Why am I pleading? This will get me nowhere.

False pity grows plentiful in kind souls, and sympathetic actions suffocate in the overgrowth.

"And what happens to me if you run away? What am I to do then?" He turns away, ashamed. Or perhaps he's annoyed.

"No one will know I went with you. I can hide. You know I can hide well. The guards at the gate won't find me, and if they do I'll say I snuck into your cart. I'd never blame you." I'm pleading with a statue. "Please just let me come?"

Aaron turns to face me and stares. His eyes linger on my scars, on the red stain across my face, on places I wish he wouldn't see. My body burns and I shudder under his watchful eyes, waiting for him to look away. Why won't he look away?

His eyes narrow with hate and disgust. "Why are you always this petulant? And you wonder why you're the one always on the ground."

———

Strange things happen in the shadows of the forest, at least that's what they always tell me. I still don't know if it's a warning or a threat. The village folk weave stories to haunt me. Stories of boogiemen who snatch you if you wander alone too late in the forest. Too far from the safety of the fire. Too close to midnight.

It's better to stay where you know the danger. Where you know you can survive. No matter what that survival costs you. For in the forest, all that lies there is unknown.

And what happens to me if you run away?

The fire sputters until it is nothing more than coals. I could throw on another log, keep the house warm while I'm gone. But if luck favors me—she never has—he'll freeze, solid and dead by the time I return.

If I return.

Aaron's words pin themselves deeper to my heart. Each day that painful, awful hope rips me apart as it tills the hidden garden filled with rotting flowers. What lays beyond the town's gate will be better than what is here. It must be. I will meet it, whatever it is.

I tiptoe around the room, searching for my boots. The thin leather does little to protect my feet, but the small semblance of warmth will keep me moving, if only I can find them. The night is cold. The dark sky holds an orange glow of a coming storm. I don't know how far I must travel to find safety. To find shelter. To find a new life. If it's even possible.

I lift every pile of refuse, searching. Nothing.

I step closer to the sleeping beast snoring in his slumber and see them. They hide behind his head for even the leather fears his wrath. He's guarding my shoes in his sleep. His hand still clutches an empty bottle, readied to be used as a weapon upon his waking.

Has he always done this? Are they kept there every night? Or did he know? Did Aaron tell him that I asked to leave?

I would have come back.

But now? I know I cannot.

I won't.

Despite the depth of his drunken stupor clutching him in sleep's grasp, I dare not risk the tide of anger. It's easier to suffer the stinging pain of the cold road ahead of me than the pain I know he will bring with him.

I tie my long black hair back at the base of my neck, the crimson silk ribbon keeping it from my face. Shame will not smother me tonight. I push the door open, slow and careful to not make a sound, grab my cloak, and escape.

The moon raises high above me as I step barefoot into the street. Freedom teases me with discomfort. It calls to me from outside the walls of this town. It keeps me focused; I choose it.

The deserted road stretches before me, unfamiliar in the dark. The shadows stretch deeper, darker than they do in the day. Faceless windows watch me with disdain, reflecting my own shame. I try not to look, not to let my gaze linger too long.

My feet carry me faster as the silver moonlight guides me, and I go.

In the distance I can see that the gate stands open. Only a single lantern lights the area. Its wicked yellow gleam stifles the gentle blue moonlight. If only it would blow out and let me pass unnoticed. But it won't.

"You there. Stop." The guard sits up as I walk past. He pauses, his dry throat swallowing hard. "You're barefoot."

I do not stop or turn to look. "I'm fine."

He grumbles as he rises to his feet. His boots are thick with sturdy soles. His feet must be so warm. "It's winter."

I shake my head and do not dare to look him in the eye. "I'm fine."

"I said to stop." His hand grabs my arm.

I swallow my scream and flail, trying to escape. Not again. I can't, not again. He pulls me toward him. His grip tightens. I did not ask for this pain.

"Stop," he repeats. The yellow lantern illuminates his sick smile. The shadows twist his face and strip away the mask, revealing his intent. He enjoys this. He pulls me into his chest, wrapping his arm around me. My face is buried in his heavy wool shirt. It itches and tears at my skin. He smells of putrid, rotten smoke and spilled ale, the same as *him*.

I claw, desperate for any escape. He laughs. He actually *laughs*. I push myself away enough to open my eyes. And I see it. I grab the dagger at his waist, slipping it silently from its sheath and I thrust it into him as he pulls me tight to him.

Again and again and again.

He does't scream.

The polished metal makes no sound as it slides through his shirt and his flesh and into his stomach. His eyes grow wide with confusion as his knees buckle. His hands slide away from me, leaving red lines of scraped flesh as he clamors for support. I give him none.

I back away, terrified. What have I done? I didn't mean to...

Did I?

Would anyone believe me?

Do I believe me?

I slip the knife into my belt and step through the gate, over the river of red blood that coalesces into the lake of sin at my feet. The white mist envelops me whole, clutching me in its protective shroud.

This. This is the world they have kept me from, and it welcomes me like a long forgotten lover.

My feet carry me further into the forest. Tall shadows of trees reach above me and stretch to the sky as the fog fades. I have no direction but I don't feel lost. The quiet excitement, the fleeting thought of freedom edges into my thoughts.

I have shed my chains.

A sea of unlimited possibilities, unbound potential, rises up and carries me away. The moonlight dances at my feet through the branches and needles of the pines surrounding me. I let it guide my path, skipping from one island of light to the next. The night air laughs at my game, gently guiding me from one path to the next. Its laughter summons a chorus of creaking from the boughs of the conifers.

A wolf howls, the high pitched yowl sends a shiver down my spine. The answers echo from all directions, the sounds distant but clear. I run, tripping over rocks I can no longer sense. And every time I make the choice to stand, to keep pushing forward. The pain is gone. My feet feel nothing as they take me further into the forest, farther away from the prison behind me.

I stumble into a tree, grasping it to keep myself from the ground. An owl hoots in frustration as its perch rustles beneath it.

A cacophony of caws answers from every direction.

Are you lost?

Shadows shift in the distance. Feverish chills grip my heart. I want to answer them, and I scream. I let go of every piece of my life I had swallowed. I am not lost, but I don't know where I'm going. This time, they answer me, closer and louder than before.

You will be safe with us.

My legs give out beneath me. No matter how hard I try, they no longer answer to my will. Snow falls and I close my eyes.

A cloud of ravens circles as the white snow falls in thick flakes.The streaks of black and white fill the air above me. They both glitter in the streaks of moonlight from above. My heart keeps time with the beat of wings. I don't know if this is fear, or excitement, but it fills me, all of me. Until that is all that remains and my world goes black.

I awake to find the ravens standing in a circle around me as I lay on the snow covered ground. They are silent, their ebony eyes peering, unblinking. But I do not mind their gaze. I push myself off the ground. I expect pain, cold, but find none.

One raven hops forward, leaving its sharp marks on the snow. It croaks once and welcomes me.

Wind rises, circling the clearing, attacking me from all sides. It carries away the ribbon tying my hair. I reach for it, unwilling to lose the one thing I still call my own. The shimmering fabric passes through my fingers and disappears into the night.

The shuffle of leather boots across the frozen ground pierces the air and the wind ceases. The cacophony of caws fills the night air and hundreds of wings take to the air. Even the birds, sure in their freedom, run from their fear and retreat to safety. I turn to run but something beneath the snow snags my foot and I plummet to the ground.

The snow drifts over me and shrouds me, sheltering me

from the approach. Each footstep is louder, nearer than the last. I lay frozen hoping they will pass. My soul need time to heal and I have not yet learned to fly.

A hand reaches down. Fingers tangle in my locks, balling into a fist as I am ripped to my feet. He breaths heavy on my neck and pulls me close, pressing my beak against his cheek. He's speaking. His mouth releases a fury of steam into the night air. I no longer understand the words.

I stare into his empty eyes, still as the storm. I do not breathe.

He throws me to the forest floor and I collapse. Pain surges though me where is breath warmed my skin. Matted black hair still tangles in his hands. He curses me, spits on me, shoves his boot on my chest.

The weight suffocates me. A shrill cry escapes me. It sounds strong, determined.

My roar echoes through the trees and fades to a silent nothingness. A moment passes. Caws, knocks and croaks answer from the trees. They come in a fury. The black swarm descends and knocks him to his back.

I scramble, scurrying away from the commotion. I watch from the base of a tree as the murder rips him apart. They start with his eyes, pecking at them as he claws, desperate to free himself from their assault. But they do not stop.

I look away. My eyes stare into the darkness. Snow glitters in the blood stained moonlight as it falls. His screams continue.

I wait for his final breath.

Silence smothers me.

A single raven caws to me. *The path is clear.* My heart pounds against my chest as I turn to look. The murder stares back at me with bloodied beaks. They hide the body from my eyes.

I push myself off the icy ground and face my freedom.

J.E. ZARNOFSKY (Salt City Genre Writers) is a writer, costumer, larper, and all around fantasy enthusiast. She always seeks new ways to tell heartfelt and collaborative stores. Apart from her day job in software, she can be observed in her natural habitats of coffee shops, ice rinks, or medieval(ish) battlefields armored and ready with her sword or bow. Follow her online at jezarnofsky.com or on Twitter @jezarnofsky.

Book Week in Utah
League of Western Writers

Yesterday marked the beginning of "book week" for Utah authors of volumes of history, fiction, philosophy, pedagogy, poetry or biography. Book sections of leading and locally owned department stores and the Deseret Book store are cooperating with the two literary leagues of the state. Books produced within the past decade are specially featured and autographed copies will be placed on sale.

Local chapters of the League of Western Writers and the National League of American Penwomen are sponsoring the movement, the purpose of which is to push reticent writers into the limelight and stimulate an interest in literature that often languishes in the presence of arts making more instant appeals to the livelier senses of sight and hearing.

The season is peculiarly appropriate for cultural associations to call attention to authors who are apt to be overlooked as prophets are said to be in their own lands. With the advent of zero weather an urge to sit in the cozy corner of a warm room and read, even the literary products of neighbors, is more potent than at any other time of the year.

Public libraries are so well stocked and so efficiently conducted these days it is a wonder that any books are sold to individuals. But there is a certain satisfaction in having a few books for company or consultation when the mood is on, and private libraries are the result.

Living with the Ultimate Sacrifice

C.H. Lindsay

No quilt
   or sunlight
   can replace
the warmth
   of his arms
   or his smile
when I wake,
   knowing my soldier
   is not coming home.

C.H. LINDSAY (Infinite Monkeys) is primarily a stay-at-home
wife and mother. She is also an actress, conrunner, poet and
writer. Of late, she spends most of her time being a hermit in
her "mom cave" where she writes and runs an online text-
based role-playing fleet of sci-fi simulations. She also collects
books. Lots and lots of books. She is a member of SFWA,
HWA, SFPA, and LUW.

WEST WRITERS PLAN ROUNDUP

Final preparations for the fourth annual Writers' round-up to be held here Saturday and Sunday were being completed Thursday by the League of Western Writers, Utah and Salt Lake chapters.

Speakers of note in the literary world are expected to start arriving Friday, it was reported by Mrs. Earl W. Harmer, general chairman of the round-up and president of the Salt Lake chapter.

The league-sponsored round-up will be held in the Art Barn, Inc., 54 Finch lane. Starting at 10 a. m. Saturday, it will feature a variety of western writers speaking on topics of literary interest.

Among the noted writers expected to attend and speak are Struthers Burt, novelist and short story author, and his wife, Kathleen Newlin Burt, fiction editor of the Ladies' Home Journal; Franklin Folsom, president of the League of American Writers, and his wife, Mary Elting Folsom, former editor of Golden Book magazine; Lexie Dean Robertson, poet laureate of Texas, and her husband, J. F. Robertson, secretary of the Rising Star, Texas, chamber of commerce, and Bennett Foster, a Texas novelist and short story author.

Approximately 100 authors and other persons engaged in literary work will participate, according to Frank C. Robertson, president of the Utah chapter of the writers' league.

Salt Lake Telegram | August 10, 1939

Merrow

Alexis Hansen

Alastar Quinn should have known something was wrong when his apprentice, Brogan Feil, claimed he heard a voice echoing across the expanse of blue waves. He didn't think anything of it later when the young man fell overboard and they had to fish him out of the water.

But then Brogan claimed he saw a woman beneath the Brazen's keel.

Everyone had heard the tales about those who dwelled in the Land Beneath the Waves, but Alastar knew them better than most, having heard them many times in all his decades. Some of the crewmen doubted the truth of these stories, evidently, because they mocked Brogan for his outrageous claim.

No one was laughing when, as the sun was dipping toward the horizon, the fisherman who thought he had snagged a shark pulled a woman on board instead.

Her hair was long and jet black, framing an otherworldly face with large, dark eyes and sharp cheekbones. Her torso was covered in mottled, scaly skin, and below that was a long and spindly tail built for speed in the open ocean.

A merrow. They were creatures of the depths, magical beings capable of changing the weather and enchanting men. In Alastar's hometown, they were known as harbingers of death.

The harpoon jutted from her fins, the tip tearing through her flesh. The men just stood there, aghast, and without thinking, Alastar rushed to kneel beside her. They needed to get her off this ship.

Her fingers were too long and tipped with pointed claws—but she didn't use them. She was eerily still and silent as he reached for the harpoon, working it out of the hole it had created.

It was difficult with the soft and slimy texture of the fins, much like the skin of an eel or seaweed washed up on shore, but he was able to remove the hook from where it was snagged.

Oily red blood oozed from her wound and the merrow pulled her tail away from his reach, eyeing him warily.

"We need to get her into the water," Alastar said, his voice hoarse. "Feil, help me get her back into the water."

But Brogan didn't move, staring at her in awe. "She's beautiful..." he whispered.

Alastar shoved the man's leg, breaking him out of his stupor. "Help me move her!"

This broke the other crewmen out of their gawking stares, and Clance—the Brazen's deck officer—yanked him away. "Are you a fool? We ain't putting her back in the water! Besides, look at her. She don't want to go."

The woman had barely moved, tail tucked close to her body and propped up on her arms so she could better see her captors. There was no fear on her face, only curiosity.

"What's the racket over here?"

A broad-chested and graying man shouldered his way through the gathered crew, but froze in his tracks at the sight of the tail that shimmered in burnished gold and sea green.

"By the Sea Mistress herself," he breathed.

"Cap'n Harver," Alastar said, pushing forward. "We need to get her back into the water, Sir. Before she spells doom for us all."

The wind picked up, humming against the surface of the ocean and bringing with it a chill.

"You spend too much time listening to the crones at port, Quinn, that's just an old wives' tale. We'll do no such thing."

"Sir, she'll bring the ocean's wrath upon us if she stays!"

His words fell on deaf ears.

"Grab a net and bring her into the officer's quarters," the captain ordered, ignoring his deck officer's protest. "Clance, you can sleep with the rest of the men till we make port. Get ready to change the sails, we're docking at the nearest port city to fetch ourselves a pretty price." When nobody moved, he yelled, "Get a move on!"

With a glare aimed in Harver's direction, Clance hurried away and returned shortly, net in tow. The merrow didn't struggle when they tossed the net over her and secured her arms to her body.

Alastar didn't fail to notice how Brogan's touch was gentle when he assisted the others in lifting her. As they carried her into the quarters, Alastar realized that the hum wasn't coming from the wind, but emanating from the merrow's throat.

Clance kept watch over his quarters, turning away all except the Captain and making no effort to be kind about it. Everyone else went back to their duties aboard the ship and work almost returned to normal, though now there was a quiet hustle of hushed whispers and suppressed excitement. No one could focus on their tasks, their thoughts instead on what was with them on the ship.

A strange energy was in the air, making Alastar's hairs stand on end. He had tried speaking with Harver again about the dangers of allowing a merrow to stay close but he was once again ignored. The Captain believed he was nothing more than a superstitious old fool, despite his years of loyal and thankless work aboard this ship.

Alastar was seven years Harver's senior, and had lived and worked on the Brazen as a shipwright for years before Captain Harver was assigned to it. He knew better than anyone how the ship worked, the feel of the wood, the creak of the masts.

He had always been looked over for his quiet nature. Now he was looked over for the gray in his beard and the stoop in his spine. He heard the whispers behind his back—that he was too old for the conditions of the job, the fast-paced work, the cramped spaces, the constant swaying and bucking of the ship that knocked crewmen off their feet.

The sea was unforgiving and the work wasn't for the faint of heart, but it was the only life he knew. There was freedom to being out on the water for months on end; even if it felt more like a prison under the command of men like Harver and Clance.

Alastar always thought he'd keep sailing until his final day, but he didn't think that day would come so soon. He didn't want the Captain's foolishness to make this their final resting place.

"Clouds are rollin' in," muttered Buck-Eye Finn, gazing out to sea. "Storm's a-coming."

Alastar grunted in response.

"The merchant flag's still up. I thought I told the Feil boy to take it down an hour ago," Finn grumbled, not deterred by Alastar's silence. "If we lose the flag during the storm, the Captain'll have his head. Maybe that'll teach the boy to not slack off."

Alastar looked over at Brogan. He was about halfway up

the rigging, watching the horizon. The setting sun painted the sky with bright reds and oranges that reflected on the water's surface, making it look as if the sea was on fire. Darkening gray clouds hung over them like smoke.

It was a breathtaking sight, one couldn't argue that, but the way Brogan was staring, it was like he couldn't even see it. Like he was in a trance.

Brogan was a good and hardworking boy, skilled with ship carpentry despite his young age. Alastar hadn't planned on taking anyone under his wing and teaching his craft, but the boy's eagerness and persistence had been difficult to refuse.

Leaving Buck-Eye Finn to his complaining, Alastar made his way over to where Brogan Feil perched on the ropes. He struggled to keep his balance, the tossing of the ship getting worse with the growing waves. On a normal evening, he would soon be able to have a nice warm dinner and retire to his hammock for the night where he would be peacefully oblivious to the Brazen's movements. But nothing about this was normal, and he had a feeling no one would be getting any sleep tonight.

"Feil!" he called up to the boy. There was no reaction, so he called again. On the third try, Brogan finally looked down at him, startled. "Come down here," Alastar ordered.

Brogan quickly did as he was told, landing deftly and with an ease that Alastar hadn't known for years. "Sir?"

"You've got a dull look in your eye. What's wrong?" When Brogan didn't answer or even acknowledge that he heard the question, Alastar grabbed his shoulders and gave him a rough shake. "Answer me, boy!"

"I need to see her," Brogan mumbled, staring at Alastar but not seeing him.

The dread that had been pooling in Alastar's gut worsened. The boy was succumbing to the merrow's spell. "She's gotten to you, hasn't she?"

"I need to see her," Feil repeated, pushing past him. "I need to hear her voice."

Alastar grabbed his arm. That damn humming hadn't stopped since they first set eyes on the merrow. Even out here, it echoed around them.

"You need to snap out of it!" he yelled. "She's enchanted you, just like she's probably enchanted half the ship by now."

Brogan saw him then, looked at him with incredulity. "You don't hear it?"

"I hear it, but I'm not about to let it take my senses away from me."

"How can you not think it's the most beautiful thing you've ever heard? How can you not need *more?*"

Alastar couldn't come up with a response. There was no reasoning with a man under an enchantment.

As the sky grew darker, the men headed into the galley to dine, more out of habit than hunger. Each of them now sported a dazed expression, and the usual conversation had ebbed away. It was like a spirit had come aboard to haunt the ship.

Alastar stayed on deck. The wind was chill, piercing through his thin clothes and numbing his fingers, but still he kept at his job, working at the surface of the wood to a perfect finish to keep it protected from seawater.

His work had been done an hour ago, but he needed something to keep his hands busy while he watched Clance stubbornly hold his post, not even getting up to eat. Whether he was going to trade places with someone else or if he would stand guard over the merrow all night, Alastar didn't know.

Eventually, Clance stood as the first raindrops began to fall. He wandered over to the port-side railing, presumably to stretch his legs.

Without hesitation, Alastar gathered his supplies as if he had just finished his job, and headed toward the galley while Clance's back was to him, turning at the last second to go into the officer's quarters.

He wasn't as quick or agile as he used to be but he knew how to keep a latch quiet when he slotted it back into place. He stayed a moment to listen through the door. If Clance returned to his post, he couldn't hear it above the sounds of water crashing against the bow.

He was in, finally—though he didn't have a plan yet for how he was going to get the merrow *out*.

Alastar knew what he was going to see in this room, but he still felt unprepared when he turned around to find the merrow's dark, inhuman eyes watching him.

The net was still draped over her, and she was curled up in the corner amid drawers overflowing with shipment records. A small lantern hung from the ceiling, swinging with the ship's movements and casting eerie shadows.

Even in the dim light, he could see the flaking of the skin on her arms, how her fins were beginning to shrivel from lack of water.

"You need to go back," he whispered, voice rough. "You—"

"Clance! Where'd you go, you useless—"

The door slammed open behind him and Alastar didn't have any time to react before a pair of fists grabbed his jacket and shoved him forward. He landed on the hard floor, his joints jolting with pain at the treatment.

"Thought you could run off with the lady, did you?" Captain Harver's hot and rancid breath was on his ear. "Thought I'd let you get away with stealing my cargo?"

He fell silent, face growing slack, and it took Alastar a moment to realize his attention was on the merrow. Her humming had become loud enough to drown out the sounds of the ocean.

"Please..." Alastar said to her from his place on the floor. "Let us go."

Her eyes fixated on him, and he could almost see a hint of confusion on her face. Her song stuttered, and that was all that was needed for the captain to snap out of it.

"I won't have someone who tries to undermine my command on my ship. At next docking, you're off the crew. Until then, you can stay locked up in here, since you're so determined to set her free." A cruel smile spread across his face. "And if your old tales about killer mermaids are correct, you'll be the first to know."

With that, he left the quarters and slammed the door shut behind him. The lock clicked into place with an echo at the same time a chorus of distant voices began.

The merrow tilted her head, listening. She hummed again, louder this time, calling to them. Her kind had come for her.

Not just her. They wouldn't leave the ship untouched. They had come for everyone.

"Won't you spare us?" he breathed.

Her eyes flicked over to him for a brief second, then she ignored him.

With a yell, he threw himself at the door, but the lock held firm. They were all doomed if they did nothing.

He shouted for Brogan, for *anyone* to let him out, shouted warnings and pleas, but no one answered. Even his yells and banging weren't enough to drown out the singing, and eventually, spent, Alastar sank to the floor.

Leaning his head against the wall, he avoided the merrow's stare. He didn't know if it was better or worse that she hadn't tried to escape.

It didn't last long, however. There was a shift in her posture, a straightening of her spine and tightening of her claws, and then she hissed, thrashing against the net. The ropes held tight, but he didn't know how much longer they would last.

Alastar tried to put more distance between them but his back was already against the door. Then he realized the singing outside had grown silent.

Moments later, the shouts of men could be heard, followed by a harsh grinding sound.

Rocks. They'd just run aground.

The Brazen lurched, sending crates and barrels crashing to the floor. Alastar was thrown to the side, and his vision blacked out.

Alastar fought through the numb cold back to consciousness and a throbbing headache. The chill sank into his bones, making his joints stiffer than they already were. He was lying face-down on top of a storage chest, water tickling his beard.

Somehow, the lantern above had only been cracked by the impact and was still burning. Though it was dimmer than before, it still illuminated the flooding officer's quarters.

The ship was sinking.

With an effort, he got to his feet. Everything ached as he sloshed through waist-high seawater, looking for the exit—only to find that the door was cracked open and outside blocking the way was part of the main mast that must have broken off.

Alastar pushed against the door but it held firm, the mast keeping it from opening enough for him to squeeze through. It was too heavy.

He was going to die in here. And with the frenzy of merrows outside—

The merrow.

His eyes darted around the space, looking for her shape in

the shadows. He'd forgotten for a moment that they were trapped in here together.

He couldn't see her. Had she escaped?

But then the water rippled and something dark slid just below the surface. A head rose up and black eyes peered up at him. She was free from the net, but was just as trapped in this room as he was. He'd been unconscious all that time. There'd been plenty of opportunity to kill him. Why hadn't she?

The head rose further, exposing her mouth with its pointed teeth—and she spoke.

"I know why my song holds no sway over you. The sea has already claimed your heart more than any woman or man ever could."

He didn't know what he'd expected her voice to sound like without the song. Beautiful and enchanting, or perhaps low and raspy. Instead, it sounded...ordinary.

Alastar didn't know what was happening outside with the rest of the crewmen, and he wasn't sure he wanted to. He could guess well enough.

"What will you do to Feil?" he asked.

Brogan had fallen so deeply under her spell, Alastar doubted his fate would be the same as the rest of theirs.

"The others won't touch him. He belongs to me, and will return with me to *Tír fo Thuinn*."

The merrows would call it a kindness to allow a human into their realm, but Alastar knew that Brogan Feil would be a slave, drifting through the rest of his life barely aware and losing himself to the depths.

The merrow swam closer, cutting through the water with ease. Alastar stiffened, ready for her to strike, but she passed by him without a glance. Bracing herself against the door blocking the way out, she pushed, straining against the weight.

It didn't budge. She hissed, then turned toward him.

"Help me."

Alastar leaned back, resting his head against the wall and rubbing his arms to try and bring out some warmth. The water level had risen up to his chest. "Why would I?"

"You will die in here if you don't."

"I will die out there if I do."

At least this way, she was stuck too.

There was silence for a moment, then, "Let us bargain. What do you want?"

He eyed her warily. "It would be foolish of me to agree to anything you offer. Your kind are notorious for tricking your way out of deals."

"But you know we have to follow a deal to the letter. Name your price. Set your own restrictions. I will not die in here with you. Your death will be quick as you drown. Mine would be slow and painful, wasting away separated from the rest of the ocean."

"Ask your merrow friends to get you out."

Her tone turned bitter. "They hold no loyalty for me."

Alastar closed his eyes and tried to repress the shivers wracking his body. "You let yourself be caught. Why?"

She paused. "I was...curious. I overestimated my ability. I thought I could easily free myself whenever I wanted."

His choices were to stay in here and drown or go out there and get torn apart. Alastar looked around. The Brazen had served him well, and it had lived up to its name. Going down with the ship wouldn't be the worst way to go. Seemed fitting, given how most of his life had been spent out at sea.

Alastar Quinn was going to die tonight, but he didn't want to end here in this small, dark room. He wanted to look out at the ocean one last time.

He straightened. "Free Brogan Feil from your spell. Let him return to land and live out the rest of his life without influence from you or your kind. Leave him be."

She frowned, thinking it over. Then she nodded. "I cannot

promise that the rest of my kind will leave him alone, but if you free me from this place, I will see him safely to land and never seek him out again."

It would have to do.

Alastar joined her, bracing himself against the door and trying to ignore the fear that made his pulse quicken from being so near an ocean predator.

They pushed in tandem, and the mast outside budged, but not far enough. Alastar struggled to pull in enough air with the water up to his chin, sputtering as he tried to push and keep his head above water at the same time.

He pulled away, gasping and coughing. He was old, his muscles couldn't take this kind of strain.

The merrow watched him, and he prepared for her to snap at him, to command him to keep going. Instead, she asked a question.

"You could have bargained for your own life. Why didn't you?" She swam closer, and he flinched as he felt her slippery tail brush his leg. "Do you view your own life as lesser because he is young and you are not? Or are you just ready to die?"

It was neither. He didn't even know why he'd asked for Brogan's safety over his own.

"I've been on one ship or another since I was old enough to scrub the deck," he said. "I've seen all manner of cruelty out on the lawless seas and turned a blind eye to it, looking out only for myself." He breathed out slowly. That was it. That was why. "I haven't done much good in my life. This is the only chance I'll have to change that."

Alastar didn't like the way she was staring at him, and he grimaced, readying himself to push again.

"We movin' this thing or what?"

She returned to her position, and he took a deep breath, lowering himself in the water to get a better angle, and shoved with all his might.

Slowly but surely, the mast moved, creating an opening.

There was a flurry of movement beside him, the whip of a tail, and Alastar pushed his way back to the surface, lungs on fire. He gasped for breath, fighting to keep himself afloat as he held onto the wall for support.

The merrow was gone, fled through the opening as soon as it was wide enough for her to fit through.

She left him here. Anger burned in Alastar's chest, though he knew it was unreasonable.

Why wouldn't she leave the second she was able? She had no obligation to stay. He wasn't part of the deal.

He didn't know if the gap was large enough for him to fit through—he wasn't as thin and lean as the merrow—but he was at least going to try.

He took a deep breath and dove, reaching blindly for the opening. His chest felt crushed in the tight space, the air forced from his lungs. Desperately, he fought his way through, clawing his way outside and up to the surface.

He made it. The sea tossed him around and he grasped desperately for some piece of the ship, latching on to part of the rigging to stop him from getting carried away. The storm was still raging and the rocks that were the downfall of the Brazen were now the only things holding it even somewhat steady. But he still made it.

His previous resignation disappeared and panic gripped his heart. He didn't want to die. Why hadn't he asked the merrow to guarantee his own safety?

A clawed and scaly hand grabbed his arm. This was it. He was about to find out what it was like to get eaten alive. Alastar jerked away, kicking out, but his legs met nothing but water.

The merrow from before surfaced beside him. Or at least he thought it was the same merrow. It was hard to tell if her features were the same in the darkness.

"The boy is near the bow, he will stay there until the storm calms," she said. "Wait here, it should subside soon. Then you can make sure he gets back to land and stays there."

He tried to blink the water out of his eyes. "You're letting me go?"

She hissed. "I can take him to shore, but it will take some time for the enchantment to fade. Without someone to keep him there, he will only try to follow me back and drown himself in the process."

She didn't wait for a response, disappearing into the dark water with a flick of her tail.

He just stared at the spot she'd occupied with incredulity. Their deal hadn't specified how she would ensure Brogan's survival, nor did they make any agreement about Alastar's fate. She was fulfilling her end of the bargain by making *him* do it. He didn't know if she just wanted to rid herself of the responsibility or if she was showing him a kindness in disguise.

Either way, if he could survive the storm and the cold and get them both back to land...he could live.

Alastar looked out at the churning water, catching glimpses of many scaled bodies breaking the surface before vanishing just as quickly. There was no sign of the rest of his shipmates...but he was still alive, and so was Brogan.

His grip tightened as he braced himself to face the next few hours battered by freezing water. He would get himself and the boy out of here. He would make sure they lived to see another day.

ALEXIS HANSEN (West Desert Wordsmiths) is a 22-year-old goatherd from Delta who's been raising goats since 2011 and writing stories for much longer than that. She was homeschooled and grew up moving from state to state across the country before finally settling down in Utah when she was thirteen. She's something of a Jack of All Trades and has done some freelancing in addition to her various jobs around the farm. Her many hobbies include writing (of course!), drawing, photography, fitness, spending time in nature, and playing with her cats. You can contact her at alh.alexish@gmail.com.

Utah Writers Organize New League In S. L.

A new organization of all Utah Writers was formed in Salt Lake City Tuesday evening at a meeting at the Art Barn. This group will be named "The League of Utah Writers" and charter members will be writers of Provo, Salt Lake City and Ogden clubs.

Frank C. Robertson of Springville conducted the meeting and a tentative constitution was drawn up to be passed upon at a later date. Election of officers will also be held in the near future.

Delegates attending from Ogden Blue Quill club were Mrs. Martha Wright, president; Mrs. Mary Knowles, vice president, and Mrs. Hortense Anderson, secretary.

The Ogden Standard-Examiner | November 5, 1939

Wholly Freed

Christopher G. Jones

I never wanted this . . .
   much freedom.
Truth is
   I loved being married.
We had 47 years of bliss,
   punctuated by
      manic cycles in which I convinced my wife
      life
      would be better in—you name a state—
         North Carolina, Utah, Massachusetts, or
         Hawaii.
"But what's wrong with California?" she would
always ask.
   "You love the beach and I love to jump waves
   on summer days."
"I have this inkling," I'd respond.
"Personal revelation?"
"Something like that."
"We're meant to go?"
"Yes."

And so, I'd schlep our family
    back and forth
    across these United States
        to discover new homes
            uncircumscribed by the 50-mile radius
            of our separate childhoods and adolescence
            at opposite ends of the greater L.A.
            metropolis.
But we always returned to base camp when it was time
    for our children to have their Nanas and Papas near
    or for us to spend the final years with aging parents.
        I lost my mother first, then
        my wife lost hers.
        Next, we both lost my dad,
            who she considered her *real* father
                because her *biological*, responsible for half
                her DNA,
                went MIA the day she was conceived.
My wife and I were orphaned now.
Our adult children and their progeny
    lived far from where we were born and raised.
So, we left the City of Angels for the sixth and final
time,
    retiring to St. George, Utah,
        wholly freed to live Life Elevated ®
        in the geographic middle,
            with half the grandkids north on I-15,
            and the other half south.
Three years later,
    my bestie, my North Star, and my lover
        with hair the color of sunsets,
    slipped
        from my fingers
            one morning

before I could hold her close
   and say,
      If love means losing my "self"
         in your embrace,
      then I'd prefer
         bondage.
Any new widower will tell you,
   total freedom is so . . .
      overrated.

Writing credits for CHRISTOPHER G. JONES (Heritage Writers Guild, The Usual Suspects) include poetry, children's fiction, general-interest magazine articles, and during his college days, financial news for the BYU Daily Universe. He is the co-author of three textbooks, over fifty professional journal articles, and a teaching novel—*Accosting the Golden Spire, 3rd ed.*

Before retiring to devote himself full-time to writing, Jones worked in public accounting and higher education, where he taught accounting, computer information systems, and business writing. He is a member of the League of Utah Writers and an affiliate member of the Mystery Writers of America.

When not penning poetry, Jones writes detective novels about surfing crime-fighter, Thaddeus Hanlon, under the pseudonym Topper Jones. Book one in the series is in final editing and will be available for agent/publisher consideration early this fall. For the latest on Christopher G., check out his website at www.topperjones.com.

WRITERS FORM CHAPTER OF STATE ASS'N. HERE

Frank C. Robertson, Springville, president of the "League of Utah Writers," was in Helper to address several aspiring writers of the county in the library, Sunday, May 12, at 2 p.m.

With Mr. Robertson was Eva Willes Wangsgaard, Ogden, first vice president, and Ed M. Tuttle, American Fork, second vice president, who came down to aid the organization of a chapter of the writer's league in this end of the state.

Mrs. Gomer Peacock, who invited the officials to be present, reported that it is really surprising how many persons throughout the county, both in Price and Helper, yearn deep in their hearts to express themselves in writing.

The league has in mind the projects of the annual "Writers' Roundup" and the writer's booth at the state fair. The league will also give writers belonging reliable information concerning agents and publishers, many of whom cheat beginning writers of thousands of dollars yearly.

Mrs. eGorge A. Schultz of Latuda was elected president, with Mrs. H. Duane Anderson of Price as secretary, the remaining officers to be chosen at the next meeting of the group next Sunday.

Helper Journal | May 16, 1940

Out of Holocaust

Grace Diane Jessen

The names of Auschwitz, Ravensbruck,
Dachau, and other camps must not
be lost, although they seem so far
away, so long ago. The thought

that horrors suffered there might be
dismissed, the words no longer read
of people starving—hoping not
for meat, but for a bite of bread—

compel us to recount the truth,
the capital offenses done
against eleven million souls.
The ones who lived have just begun

to tell their wrenching tales, of how
their clothes, their dignity, their hair
were taken; how a guard could beat
a person for no cause, could pare

his hope and pride to nothing, force
the weak to stand for hours in cold,
to sleep with three per narrow cot,
no mattress, but with lice and mold.

The Prince of Darkness ruled the land
too long, but some survived to see
the death camp gates swing wide,
to walk away, alive and free.

GRACE DIANE JESSEN (Sevier Valley Chapter) is an
honorary lifetime member of the League of Utah Writers.
She is also a member of the Utah State Poetry Society. She
has received many awards for her poetry in state and national
contests and many of her poems have been published. She
recently enjoyed the challenge from Salt Lake Community
College to write 30 poems in 30 days and received honorable
mention for her collection. She lives with her husband Gordon
in Glenwood, Utah, where they raised their seven daughters.
They also have 18 grandchildren.

Freeing You

Kam Hadley

"I will free you," I said in my head.
I will free you and forgive.
You hurt me, but I'm moving on.
I'm letting go, this load of lead.

I set down my stones and walked away.
I couldn't believe how it felt.
A weight had lifted off my chest.
I'd been unshackled today.

It didn't mean what happened was right.
It wasn't all okay.
So, I handed off my burden,
Allowing in the light.

I thought that I was freeing you,
By letting this all go.
But, forgiveness is more than this,
And the blessings are just huge.

This clemency to liberate you,
Has rather, instead, freed me.
You may continue as before,
But I begin now, anew.

KAM HADLEY (Blue Quills) writes poetry and short stories.
Find Kam on Twitter @kamhadleywrites.

In the Shadow of the Mountain

Chris Jones

We had a Pull to one of the old towns, a ratty tavern none of us remembered, and it cost us far more than we thought it would. Nearly everything, actually, which when you have little to begin with, is painful and not a little terrifying —emotions we thought we'd left behind.

The Pull came with the sunset, as it often does, the red glow of the sun fading behind the oak- and ash-clad hills. It brought on the gloaming and that release back into some semblance of the life we once enjoyed. To be rooted to the grave, to the nightly reminder of the grisly remains of the time before, left little in the way of sensory enjoyment, but we could still—some more than others—hear the nightjar's cry as it rolled over the downs, feel the thin wisp of the twitching breeze across the close-cropped grass and between the headstones, sniff the rotsmell—not unpleasant—of the leaves and the worms and the bones, and even taste the still-sharp tang of the last meal, quite long ago for some of us now.

Most nights, as the dark creeps over the cemetery, the only Pull is to the air and the mist, which often creeps up ghostlike —ironically—from the chuckle of the brook at the bottom of the graveyard hill. It is better than the damp of the box. Most of ours have melded to the soil now, and the dirt crowds in. It matters little. We take up little enough space now.

But this night, even before the last of the orange faded to gray in the western sky, we all felt it calling—the Pull. Someone somewhere thought on us, and remembered, and perhaps—the Pull was strong enough—spoke of us. Remembering is weak stuff, thin like watered gruel, but speaking, the telling of our stories—that grips like talons in the chest. It drew us forth, yanked us from our dreary peace, and our shades tramped over the dewdraped ground before the stars came to greet us.

"Grinstead. You're up early," I said, seeing the tattered dregs of his old uniform drag themselves loose from underneath the plinth.

"Cap'n," he said, nodding. "Always here, you are."

"Always will be," I said, drawing off my tricorn cap, inspecting it, and replacing it, lest someone make a crack about—

"Thought you'd get your hair back, Cap'n, no offense." Behind me, a cough, and a shuffle of boots. No one could have heard it but we, the few of the troop that remained. None of us *remained*, of course, yet here some of us were. Abimael Moorcock, for instance, my sergeant, balder than the mown top of a wheat field.

"It hasn't happened for you, either," I said.

"Ah, that's because I never had any to start with," he said. "Bald from birth, that's me."

Comforting it was, this patter, the back and forth that we'd made so often before. It made the stiff of the dusk less oppressive. Soon full night would restore us, insofar as we could be restored.

Eleven, tonight. Eleven forms, wisplike and pale in what remained of the light.

"'Twas eighteen, time before," said Abimael.

"Lost Collins and vanBeek at the tavern."

"Caught the light. Aye."

"And the rest—"

"Faded. Aye. Went On, like."

Perhaps we would go On, too, but tonight there was work for us, what remained of the Virginia Carolina Militia, so far from home.

The source of the Pull was not close, I could tell. How far, I could not say, but it was far, and yet the strength of it was beyond anything I had felt recently. Perhaps ever. Well, at least since Penelope laid down to rest. She did not linger as I did, but there was perhaps less to keep her here. The children— Peter, Francis, Maybelle—all had gone, and the grandchildren were few and distant; they knew her hardly at all, by letters a bit, but not in person, and they would not have reached out. Me, even the children remembered only as a vague shadow, marching away up the Spotsylvanie road, never to return. Penelope had been long gone now...so long. I felt her Pull, too, constant and sweet, and one day I would go to it, give in and go On, but today was not that day.

The raggedy eleven arrayed themselves in front of me in a loose line, like a string snapped and lying slack.

"Attention!" Abimael barked, and the line tautened. Shoulders came back, eyes snapped front, hands grasped for weapons that no longer existed, long since having become one with the loam and the clay. Yet the discipline held. We were yet something of what we once had been.

Abimael looked to me. "Cap'n?" he said, eyes sliding in the direction he knew we should go. A good sergeant, Abimael. He made me look like a much better captain than I ever was or would have been.

"Left face," I said, keeping the weariness from my voice. The line of faces turned ninety degrees, toward the northwest. "For'ard, harch." The line moved out smartly over the smooth ground of the cemetery, down the remainder of what once was a considerable hill. We could clearly see the headstones, trees, decorative obelisks, crypts, and so on, if we chose. Those existed for us, and wading through them was painful. But also, like a sort of film on glass, we saw what once was—the forest that had occupied this hill the last time we were a company. We did not have to obey those laws, not at all, but we instinctively bent our way to miss the thick oak trunks, for they were just as real in our minds as that which occupied this plane now.

Abimael led the troop, head on a swivel, as if he might come across one of Gage's raiding parties. If I remembered my long-rotted, hastily scribbled map, Waco, the town—such as it was—lay in this direction, through heavily brambled and wooded Carolina. It might be a long march indeed, from Mountain Rest Cemetery to the little town. If the Pull came from there, and not somewhere beyond. There hadn't been much in Waco the last time I had visited.

Which was...when?

"Knewstubb," I said, getting the attention of the third man in line, the quartermaster. "What year is it?"

Knewstubb swallowed, the white of his throat stark against the dark trunks of the maples. "No idea, Cap'n, sir," he said.

"Well," I said, a bit gentler, "When was it the last time we marched?"

"1805, sir," he said.

I grunted. I remembered that march, east, to a small commemorative gathering in the relatively larger town of Gastonia. Twenty-fifth anniversary. And some stories were told, and the place was thick with the Remnant, cheering and reminiscing; crying ghostly, insubstantial tears that some still knew what we had done here.

But that was long ago. I felt it in the weariness and too-stretched substance of what remained of my form as if I were an old shirt laid in a chest for years, stiff and brittle when finally brought out, scratchy on the skin and fraying at the folds. I rubbed at myself, and the feeling eased a bit. A few miles of marching would cure it, I hoped.

The fellows—good fellows all, that fell on the side of that mountain—seemed troubled in much the same way. They marched badly, but they had always marched badly. What they had done well was shoot like the very devil; long Kentucky rifles flaring out in the dusk and picking the hats off the British at a half mile and more. I could smell the gunpowder, and the ring of the ears after a staggered volley lingered still in my hearing.

The moon—a day or two before full—rose behind us and the light was welcome. Though we were creatures of the night, we craved darkness only for our safety and security, not for love of it. The bright of the sun would burn us to nothing, but the light of the moon soothed like a warm bath. Here and there a smile lit the face of one of the men, and my own lips turned up a fraction. We marched more easily.

But marching through woodland makes no good time, and there were no roads that led from our resting place to the restlessness that drew us on, so our line frayed, fractured, fell apart, and we marched loosely abreast, keeping the moon to our rear right-hand quarter, and the watchful eye of the sergeant to the left and the captain to the right was enough to ensure the pace didn't slacken overly.

Ghosts we might be. But we were still soldiers.

Ah, the lovely country. Virginia stands alone in the beauties that God bestowed on the earth, but He clearly had a good bit of loveliness left over to smear into the hills of Carolina. Dogwoods, just in bloom, pinks and whites and almost silvers, winked their broad eyes at us as we passed. Above, the stars shone through the lace-leaf of the canopy. I'd have shied a stone just to feel the motion of it, but no stone would come to my hand—not simply for the asking. A man would try for it, now and then—inhale the air as if his lungs were still capable of it, kick at the rough, leaf-strewn soil, though it made no scuff in the flat matted undergrowth. It was what we would have done, years back. We knew no other way.

We had marched a good while—an hour or more, by the moon—when Marscall drifted toward me like a branch of a creek diverted by a bar of sand, letting his path float nearer until we were side by side.

"Eleven of us, Cap'n," he said, a quaver in his voice.

"Ayup."

"There were more, once, weren't there?"

I looked at him. "You don't remember?"

He screwed up his face for ten paces or so. "I do...but not clearly. I can remember a bigger company, but the faces are faded and lost. You know?" He glanced over quickly to see if I did, and relaxed when I nodded.

I did know of what he spoke, though to me every face was still sharp as the day it had been that morning in the rising sun as we faced the mountain, poured powder and rammed shot, and crept through the thickness of the woods toward the enemy, whom we expected to be dug in and waiting.

Fifty-six men. My own men. Thirty-one laid down that day, and buried not far from where they fell. Where *we* fell.

"You, uh, you remember them, don't you?" Marscall said.

"Every one."

"Do they pull on you?" He left his gaze on my face this time.

"They do."

"They calling you On?"

I barked a laugh, with no mirth in it. "Some. But there are those here, keeping me close. And sometimes, a few remember. That stirs the blood."

He looked me up and down, eyebrows raised. I said, "You know what I mean."

His turn to nod. "Not so many of us, now, keeping you here. You had a wife. She calls you, too, I bet."

"For you it's…" I tried to remember. He'd been so young— first combat. First days in the company, in the backcountry. But he could shoot the eye out of a bird on the wing. "A brother?"

He beamed. "Robert. My twin brother."

"What happened to him?" I said.

He shrugged. "How could I know? He was alive when…when…that day." He ran a hand through his long, dark hair. He was a half head shorter than I, not yet entirely grown, and never would be. "But now, he calls On," he said. "How- ever he died, he don't linger."

"And you're asking me if it's all right for you to go."

He looked away. "Beg pardon, Cap'n. Not my place."

"Look at us, Marscall. James. We're little but the remnants of things that have long since ceased. I can no more keep you here than cause the sun to fail to rise."

"But I swore an oath," he said, his voice shaking, longing, but still dutiful.

Ah yes. The oath. And we had kept it. In life, in death. We kept it still.

I put an arm on his shoulder. To me, it felt the same as if he were standing there in the cool October sunshine. "And ye've kept it," I said. "None can say aught against you."

"Not you, Cap'n? Not at the Judgment?"

"Nay, son. Not I. Ye've kept faith."

Something went out of him, then, a little tension or rigidity or knotting of the muscles, ropy and sinuous under the thin shirt. "Cap'n, what is On?"

He and I kept stride, rounding a boulder and jogging down a slight dip to wade through a creek and up the opposite bank. He reached back for me, gave me his arm to cling to. We marched forward, the line to our left, ragged but united.

"I don't know," I said, finally.

None of us did. And that as much as anything kept us from going.

We marched up a long, shallow rise to the top of a substantial hill, and there in the valley twinkled the firelights of four or five houses clustered around a better-lit structure, probably a tavern or inn of some kind. The Pull, which had been strengthening and thickening throughout the march, now tore at us like a mighty wind, as if it would lift us off the hill and drop us in the valley below. Alas, no such speedy transit was vouchsafed us. Even in death, it was march or lie down and die.

We marched. The hill was slick with dew and half-rotted leaf, and the ground loamy and laced with sand, giving our boots no purchase. It maddened that we were unable to affect the leaves and pebbles of the ground beneath us, yet their character somehow transmitted itself to our gear and made footing treacherous. We fell. Vivion didn't even try to hold himself up —not that it would have helped—but went rolling down the hill to the base. He picked himself up a hundred feet below us and dusted himself off as if any of the soil could have clung to his ridiculous oversized coat.

"Hu, Vivion! You hurt?" called out Abimael, and the answer was a laugh that echoed off the hill.

"Nay," he said eventually, checking himself over. "It's as if I be dead already."

"Har," said Abimael, jogging down the last few feet. The company formed around him. He looked to me, and I nodded. It was open field from the hill's base to the edge of the houses, and we would march it like regulars, though we had never been allowed that lofty status.

"Ten-shun! Form line!" Abimael said, not needing to yell.

The line dressed as if on parade. I went down it. Rockhould. Jones. Marscall, Vivion, Blissit, half a dozen others. My friends.

"For'ard," I said, and the line moved out smartly. I was

proud of them—newly proud on every march. Ragged militia, they called us, not worth a rifle. But we had been. We showed our quality. Just the one time, but once was enough when it was all we had.

The houses sat small and wan around a central square— also small but well-tended, with grass in the center and a graveled path on each side. At the far end, north, squatted the inn that was the source of the Pull, now strong like the noon sun with nothing to obscure it. Lamplight shone from inside the wide front doors, which stood open though the evening was acquiring a chill. Two hundred yards before we reached it, a gale of laughter poured out like an incoming tide. The Pull was so strong it lifted me off my feet.

"At the double!" I said, and we ran, our feet barely touching the earth.

At the front doors I halted the company and peered in one side, with Abimael gaping through the broad front window to his left. "Full of custom," he said.

From my vantage, too, there were hardly any spaces available in the place. We could stand in the same space as a living being, but it would do us no good, and the sensation seemed unpleasant to them as well. Fortunately, there were other ways.

"Up," I said, and pointed to the roof, tiled in ceramics and in excellent repair. But that wouldn't hinder us. And there were rafters up there on which we could sit. Room for all of us, and no danger should we fall. What could we break or bruise?

We went up in militia fashion, Pelley leading the way monkey-like, and drawing the rest of us up afterward. We disliked passing through something meant to keep things out, but the nausea passed and we were inside, above the candelabras that lit the interior. And then I saw what had drawn us there.

Campbell. That was William Campell, or I was General Washington's horse.

I forgot to sit down, for a long time. William Campbell was the reason I was there. Had been there. Had fought, and taken a ball in the shoulder that was meant for Vivion, another in the leg that had passed through a tree trunk, and a final spike of steel in the upper chest from a filthy private that had claimed to be surrendering.

That private was buried in our same cemetery, his grave containing what was left of his body after twelve men gave him Tarleton's quarter following his murder of me. He had gone On within minutes, after we made it clear we would be hounding him beyond the grave. There were a lot more of their men than there were of ours, but on our own ground it was no contest. If we were thin like a worn curtain, they were the low mist of morning, so thin they might not have been there at all.

Campbell.

His hair lay long and gray along his still-broad shoulders, and rheumy eyes stared from behind thick spectacles, his hands shook except when holding a full tankard, and his voice was raspy like a file, but it was *Campbell*, sure enough, thicker than two oaks grown together and with a mind like a bear trap.

"Morning of October 7, it was, in 1780. Most of you not even born then, I shouldn't wonder, and yet you're here because we were there that day." He pointed, back over the hills to the mountain, and the place we fell.

"Gage's men were running, and an Irishman had the company here, a thousand or more, camped on the side of King's Mountain, spread like a blanket right to the top."

Thirty, forty men crowded in upon him, as if his tale were unknown to them. And perhaps it was. They were most of them young men, not above thirty winters, and the War of the Revolution was ancient to them, like the wars of the Romans and Greeks.

"We were quiet, we men of Virginia, and we crept up on

them so silently we could have eaten their breakfast right from their own pots. By the time we began firing we didn't need to be crack shots. Down went the officers, bang!" he said, standing abruptly. His voice cracked out like a shot.

"And down went the men! They screamed like sheep at the slaughterhouse, and ran, but where could they run, with the Carolinians to one side and the devils of Virginny to the other? So they ran up the mountain, trapped like goats. It was a massacre." He paused, and drained half his tankard. He always had a belly for ale like a river's run.

"But there was one man—he was a canny bastard. Ferguson, said his name was. His men stood about him like a wall, and gave back shot for shot. Down went Cooksey to my right, and Douglass to my left, and a ball passed through my cloak, whining like a lost soul." He pulled open his old coat then, and his meaty finger stuck through from one side to the other. The men leaned in to get a better look, and some stood on tables.

We were as captivated as they. We, who had been there. My company sat on thick oak roof-beams and gazed down in rapt attention.

"His men gave as good as they got for nigh an hour. They might have punched a hole in the line then, and leaked out the wineskin, but they were up against Virginny boys, and not just any company, neither, but Wheeler's boys, fresh from the farms and filled with piss." He drained the tankard, and suddenly all my men were looking at me.

"Makepeace Wheeler, his name was. A captain," said Campbell, "and he had a sergeant, too, a big cuss with a scar as wide as the Rappahannock, and some godawful name like Abimelech. No, Abimael!" He slapped his meaty thigh. "Abimael Moorcock. He led the men into shot and shell like the fist of the Almighty, and when they come out, half were dead. Captain Wheeler was shot twice, and still dragged his leg and shoulder up the hill into hellfire. Would have lived, too, but he was a gentleman, though he'd laugh to hear me say it. A lice-ridden private held up a hand and asked quarter, and Wheeler, he lifted his pistol, when the man rammed a bayonet into his chest. We gave the stinking redcoat to his Maker that day, and may he be greeted by the fires of eternal torment, amen!"

"Amen!" boomed out the answer. Tankards were raised, and drunk from. All drank to the damnation of that poor private. I nodded to my men, pantomiming the same, some making even more obscene gestures. I fought down a laugh.

We were visible, I realized with wonder.

Spirits walk all about the earth, and few can see them, but there are those that call so strongly, whose Pull is so great that they feed us substance, until our outlines take on color and heft. To my eyes, the bald head of Abimael was tinged in red now, and the butternut breeches of Gahoole showed yellow against the smokedark beams. If they look up, I thought . . . if they look, they will see us.

It was a thing that had never happened. But Campbell was that kind of talespinner. A maker of true magic.

"And that was the Battle of King's Mountain. Hailed across the colonies as the day the war turned for General Washington and LaFayette and the Fathers of our Freedom. And here you sit, not an hour's easy walk from the Mountain, and you should be glad every day for the brave bones that lie on the side of the hill.

"A toast, my new friends, to the iron of the men gone by! May they never be forgotten!"

Mugs and tankards were raised, and the cheer was so loud it rocked us on our perches.

And Campbell looked up, tipping his head to drain his cider.

His eyes could hardly have seen ten feet, but I caught the expression on his face as his filmy orbs locked on to mine. His jaw went slack in recognition. I could do nothing but nod. He nodded back, his frame shaken by backslaps and gladhanding, tankards thrust in his direction as if it were a great honor for him to drink another flagon of their brew.

Without taking his eyes from the rafters, he held up a hand for quiet.

"They're here," he said. "They're here—the men of Virginia."

The din was a while in quieting, but quiet it did. By then, we had all risen from our perches to stand, arrayed in a square on the beams around the central candelabra, with firelight playing on our faces, so strong was the Pull of the place and the time and the mighty hero that invoked us.

"Makepeace Wheeler," he said, his voice a whisper that carried yet to every corner of that house. His eyes moved left, and he said, "Abimael Moorcock." The sergeant nodded to him. The ancient eyes, unseeing yet seeing us as clearly as they had that morning he'd sent us into fire urging us to "fight like devils."

He named us all, one by one, his gaze traveling from one face to another, and tears poured like runnels down the sorrow-lines of his weathered face. "James Marscall. Honorable Gahoole. Phineas Pelley. Nathan Vivion." My men said their honorable names, and Colonel William Campbell honored them with his voice and his weeping, and then all wept, for they could not see us, though they looked, too, but they knew that the old colonel could.

They knew what we did not. For they had far more experience with death than we, though we had ourselves been through the door. Once through it, we saw little more, but these had seen it close, and some knew that the old colonel was approaching the portal, and reaching out his hand. Maybe that is why he could see us so well. I don't know.

He finished his roll call of praise and thanks, and bowed his head. "May God have mercy on their souls, and send them on to dwell with Him on high, amen," he said.

Marscall was gone before the echo of his voice had died out. I was looking at him, and then he faded like the light from a room when a candle gutters to its last bit of wick. Two others, Gahoole and Knewstubb, saluted me smartly and passed out through the roof. I never saw them again.

I knew it for the end, then, though my unbeating heart would not admit it.

Campbell, upright as a driven post throughout the night, slumped suddenly into his chair as a marionette with cut strings. Alarmed, the men tried to rouse him, but he remained insensible.

As if waiting for that signal, the cock crew.

My remaining men, the eight of us, stared at me in alarm. It could not be that late. It could not. How could so many hours have passed and left us?

For a shade, such as we, the tethering to the place of the last rites is very strong. It gives us our substance, such as it is. In the ferocious light of day we have no mass—it is burned from us like the dew from the grass. Only in the cooldark of the gravesite can our thin apparitions remain from night to night. To be caught in the sun's rising is to be sent On, whether one wills or no.

The Pull vanished with the ending of Campbell's consciousness. We were free, and we ran.

Abimael was never very fast, and his barrel-torso sported only vestigial legs. He could pull like a plough-horse, but run no faster than a waddling goose. He was only to the base of the steep hill when the light grew so strong it began to hurt our eyes. The rest of the troop was halfway up the hill and making for the trees, which might provide some shade, perhaps allow them to get back to safety. Their eyes implored me, as I stood at the base of the hill, and they called on me to come on, I could still make it if I hurried.

But I knew I could not. And I would not, not without my oldest and dearest friend.

"Go," I said to them. "I release you from your oath to me, and with all my friendship bid you farewell. Perhaps, my friends, we shall meet again. If not, then know that from the depth of my heart I honor and love you all."

They stared, and snapped a salute to me. Then they vanished over the rise.

I put out my hand for Abimael. "Come, old friend. Let us climb one more hill together."

There was just time. The sun's blaze fired the tops of the trees above us as we took the last halting step and stood looking down on the little town. Men scurried about, and women, too, carrying hot water and blankets and shouting for hurry, that they could still save him, but I knew there was no need.

For outside the tavern stood a young man, whose straight-backed stance and thick, dark hair under a tricorne hat I knew as if it had been yesterday and not thirty years before. He was wispy and transparent in the rising light, but he shone like a star. His eyes fixed on us, and his hand came up, ramrod straight, to meet his eyes.

We snapped to attention and returned the salute, in time to see him vanish. Then we turned east, toward the fatal sun.

Abimael said, "If we get to the base beyond the hill, there be dark there an hour or so longer."

I shook my head. "One more time, I want the sun in my eyes."

He drew off his hat and held it, his face toward the east. "Aye. I was wantin' to go On, meself."

I glanced at him. "Together, then."

"Jeanne be glad of you, after all this time," he said, clearing his throat.

I laughed. "She'll be pleased to meet you."

The merciful rays of the sun burned like a brand. But not for long.

CHRISTOPHER JH JONES (Utah Valley Legends), after decades without success, quit writing in 2013. After trying repeatedly to grow up—without discernible success—he repented, and has gone on to publish several books in multiple genres. He is known for his business book, *From Poop Into Gold: The Marketing Magic of Harmon Brothers*, and other nonfiction titles; for his true-crime historical thriller series *Trinity Flynn;* and for *Twelve Upon a Time*, his collection of original fairy tales. A prolific writer of short fiction as well, Cj has published two short-story collections and this is his seventh anthology.

His latest labor of love is founding Drabatic Press (drabaticpress.com). We're all still waiting to see how that turns out.

Cj resides in Lehi, UT, with his wife Jeanette, their eight children, three children-in-law, one murderous cat, and a stray hummingbird. He loves Twitter, (@christophjhj), Instagram (@alsochrisjones) and visitors to his website (iamchrisjones.com).

Carpool Meditation

Valarie Schenk

I caught it today.
Hope.
It tumbled,
unexpectedly,
through my open car window
as I sat,
waiting,
taking in rich fall colors,
storing them mentally
to stave off the bitterness
of an anticipated long, cold winter.
The warmth
of sunshine covered my forearm.
I glanced down to catch freckles
erupting on a pallor of tired skin,
when a puff of coolness
interrupted my thoughts.
That's when it happened:
once forsaken hope
presented in the form

of a delicate, floating seed,
a refugee,
having escaped the tight cell of a
milkweed seedpod.
It perched resolutely
on the peak of my upturned knee.
The contrast of white fluff on indigo denim,
stretched taught,
impenetrable,
struck me.
Then,
before I could muster pity for its unfruitful landing,
I set it free.
It took off,
sky-bound,
with unfettered resilience,
to continue its journey
to fertile ground.
And deep within me,
a seed of hope was planted.

VALARIE SCHENK (Blue Quill) is a creative based in Roy, Utah who serves through art and writing in order to assign meaning to personal experiences and communicate lessons learned through living. It is her deepest desire that these efforts promote and create safe spaces where people can connect with one another and heal alongside a friend. Learn more about Valarie on Instagram at @valarieschenk5898 or search her name on Facebook.

Autograph

Anna Bessesen

It's hour four of the signing and Annie's hand is starting to cramp. She's just finished up asking her agent to cut the line off after these last few fans when she hears the voice piping up from in front of her.

"Thank you."

Annie is used to people that only know her as an actress gushing over her, focusing on her roles and her brilliance and her beauty. She's used to the people that see the confidence she wants them to see instead of the constant fear and worry in her chest. Something tells her this isn't going to be one of those times.

She smiles up at the girl and plasters on the press smile that never makes it more than skin deep. "Of course," she says, smothering her drawl as much as she can. It's gotten easier over the years. Dani still teases her about it when—

Annie cuts that thought off at the pass. She glances at the glossy photo the girl's got in her trembling fingers. It's from one of her older movies, just a few years after she'd started on hormones and taken Dani's last name.

"Who should I make it out to?"

The girl's lips twist into a grimace before she stands up a little taller. "Cassie," she says, voice taut in a way that has Annie sitting up straight. She doesn't need to look down at the girl's badge to know there's a different name on it. There's a flash of tension in her chest, tight and sudden, and she isn't quite sure how to wrangle it.

Cassie stares back at her, dark eyes bright and defiant. There's no hint of a blush in her dark skin, but there is something about Cassie's expression that leaves Annie somewhere between elated and nauseated. She exhales slowly, trying not to let her nerves show. She fixes her media smile back in place. "Of course." She holds out a hand for the photo. Cassie's fingers twitch, and the photo paper crinkles. Annie can see it now, the too-heavy makeup and the too-careful placement of her clothes. It shouldn't be so obvious.

Slowly, Cassie holds the photo out to her. Annie doesn't snatch it from her fingers, moving slow and steady instead as she takes it between thumb and forefinger. Cassie bites her lip and, after a moment, releases it. Annie smiles back at her, staring down at the unfamiliar features on the photo before her. It's jarring to see so much of Cassie reflected in this not-so-ancient vision of herself. She swallows past the thickness in her throat and starts to grab her usual silver sharpie.

At the last second, she stills. Pink. Pale pink. Baby blue too, if she's got it.

She glances up at Cassie. The hope in her eyes is impossible to deny.

Annie smiles at her. "Just one sec." Cassie blinks, but Annie doesn't let herself linger. Instead, she goes for her purse and pulls out exactly the sharpie she'd had in mind. The inscription comes in the space of a breath.

She smiles up at Cassie, one of the real ones that she usually saves for Dani. Cassie's face lights up, and she reaches for the photo. "Thank you." The words are breathless and hopeful and tighten something in Annie's throat.

"No," Annie says. "Thank _you_."

A smile splits Cassie's face wide, and there's no denying that that will be the highlight of Annie's day. Possibly her week. She almost wishes she'd taken a second to snap a photo with the girl, but then, that might have been a bit too much with how nervous Cassie had been. Besides, if their paths are meant to cross again, they will.

Annie made damn sure of that.

To Cassie
Thank you for reminding me why I do what I do.
You're going to change the world. Don't let it change you.
You know where to find me if it tries.
Annie

ANNA BESSESEN (Infinite Monkeys, Salt City Genre Writers) is a queer transformative fiction author and a lifelong learner. She has spent two decades putting pen to paper, first as a poet and later venturing into prose. When she isn't throwing words at the page, Anna is a National Board Certified Teacher that spends her days trying to teach math to teenagers despite the fact that they seem to be more interested in the life lessons she teaches than in math.

Organization of New Society Heads Carbon Club Events

PRICE—Organization of the fourth chapter of the League of Utah Writers was effected in Price recently, when Frank C. Robertson of Springville, president of the state league; Edward R. Tuttle of American Fork, state president of the organization, and Mrs. Robertson met with eastern Utah writers at the Helper library.

Mrs. George A. Schultz of Latuda was elected president of the local group, which will be known as the Eastern Utah chapter, League of Utah Writers. Lamont Johnson of Huntington was named first vice president; Mrs. Lowell E. Barker, Price, second vice president, and Mrs. H. Duane Anderson, Price, secretary-treasurer. Lowell F. Barker was appointed publicity chairman, and Mrs. Gomer P. Peacock chairman of membership in Price, with Mrs. Grace Van Werven, membership chairman in Helper.

Meetings of the organization will be held regularly on the second Sunday of each month.

will be Miss Louise Hills, invitations; Miss Helen Lee, program; Miss Marian Clay, decorations, and Miss BeverLee Hills, refreshments.

Price Woman's club closed the current club year with a beautifully appointed tea at the municipal clubroom Wednesday afternoon under direction of Mrs. Parley H. Rhead, Mrs. Henry Pace and Mrs. J. R. MacKnight.

Mnemomic club members were guests of Mrs. Melvin C. Wilson on Friday at dinner and sewing. Mrs. George E. Jorgensen gave a review of Dorothy Canfield Fisher's "The Bent Twig."

Members of the Social Sewing club met at the home of Mr. and Mrs. Bert Bunnel at Helper, inviting their husbands to participate in a house warming in honor of the hostess.

Mr. and Mrs. Hal G. MacKnight were hosts to members of the Sunday Breakfast club at Scofield this week. A campfire breakfast was enjoyed, and

Gilded Cages

J. Milligan

T he birdcage was new.

I knew all the rooms in the duchess's estate inside and out. I knew the placement of everything, from the largest piece of furniture to the smallest curios on the mantel. I knew the exact angle to turn the decanter so the duchess didn't have to adjust it when she reached for it after she finished checking the day's ledgers. I had cleaned this room a thousand times and more.

It had never held a birdcage. The duchess did not approve of keeping pets. Least of all noisy, messy, useless creatures. Like birds.

I crept closer, curious despite myself.

The cage was ornate and heavy. It sat in the precise center of a small table that was also a new addition to the study. Aside from a single swing, there was nothing inside the cage. No dishes for food or water. No lining in the bottom. Maybe there wasn't a bird at all.

Of course not. I should have known. The cage's occupant was a tiny man. A *winged* man.

I sucked in a sharp breath and stumbled back two hasty

steps. The duchess had caught and caged one of the fair-folk. A fairy.

It wasn't an impossible thing, but it was foolish. All fairies had great magic, and their greatest, most dangerous magic of all was the giving of wishes.

"Be careful what you wish for," my mother often said. "You never know when one of the fair-folk might be listening, and they never give you what you might expect."

I waited, thready pulse in my throat, but the winged man didn't so much as twitch. I let out a quavering breath, then turned my focus back to the job at hand, where it belonged. I worked quickly, but quietly, afraid of attracting the fairy's attention.

On my way out, I hesitated. Before prudence could reassert itself, I spun around and curtsied at the fairy's back, then hurried on my way.

That afternoon, the duchess struck me across the face when I bumbled into her path. At least she hadn't been armed with her riding crop.

I spent the rest of the day peeking around every corner and doorway to reassure myself the duchess was somewhere else.

"Who hit you?"

I startled hard enough to wrench something in my back. I bit my lip to stifle a whimper. Dragging my gaze to the gilded cage, I found the fairy staring straight at me. I tightened my grip on the broom handle, as if it could shield me from the monstrous magic of the fair-folk.

"You did not wear a bruise yesterday," the fairy said. When

he spoke, it sounded like music. Sweet and lilting, comforting as a mama's lullaby. "So who, then, hit you?"

I shook my head, bewildered. "Why do you care?"

I could have—*should have*—bitten my tongue. What was I thinking, talking to a fairy? Talking to the *duchess's* fairy. If she learned of it…

"I suppose I shouldn't," the fairy said. He shifted on his perch, making it swing. "Do you not pity the bird with the broken wing? Or the limping rabbit?"

Speaking once was an accident, likely to be forgiven. Speaking again would be a mistake.

"I do," I said.

He flicked his wings. "It is the same."

Being compared to a wounded animal made me feel small and weak. I also found I didn't care for his pity. It ignited a tiny ember of…something. Anger, maybe, though that was danger-ous. Anger would get me fired or worse if expressed at the wrong time, to the wrong person.

"It doesn't matter," I said.

I pointedly turned my back on him and continued my sweeping, determined not to speak to him again.

"Take this to the duchess."

Grandine, the head housekeeper, shoved the tea tray at me, giving me no choice but to catch it or drop it.

"But I don't usually—"

"Anna has yet to come in," Grandine said, talking over me. "The other girls are busy. You'll have to do. Now go. Don't let the tea cool."

I said the only thing I could. "Yes, ma'am."

Each quick step I took closer to the duchess made my heart pound harder. My palms grew slick with sweat, and I nearly dropped the tray. By some miracle, I didn't spill a single drop of tea.

I paused outside the study door, took a deep breath, knocked—a soft tap designed not to draw attention—and then entered.

The duchess stood before the fairy's cage, her back to the doors and hands clasped behind her. Her shoulders blocked my view of the fairy in the cage, but I had no doubt he was there.

"—*will* give me what I want," the duchess was saying.

I kept my head down as I carried the tray to the sideboard and began fixing a cup. My hands shook, clattering teacup against saucer, and I winced.

"I will not," the fairy said, his voice carrying over the small sound of porcelain on porcelain. "No matter how long you keep me confined. No matter what horrors you inflict on me, I will not give you my name. I'll not grant you so much as a single a wish."

The duchess remained still, except for the clenching of her hands, which the fairy could not see.

I went still, too, but it wasn't anger that held me, like it did the duchess. It was horror. Everyone knew fairy names had power. Learn a fairy's true name, and you gained control of the fairy's magic. If the duchess learned his name, the fairy wouldn't be limited to granting her three wishes. He would have to give the duchess whatever she wanted, without question or hesitation or bargaining.

The duchess was young and vain. She was jealous. And she hungered for power, even though she was the single most powerful woman in the kingdom. The thought of the duchess with a fairy's unfettered magic at her command chilled me to the core.

No. Don't think about it. Just do what must be done and go.

After trying to still the trembling in my fingers, and failing,

I carefully picked up the teacup and saucer and carried it to the table the fairy's cage perched on. I wasn't as confident about the correct placement of a fresh cup of tea as I was a decanter of brandy, but I made my best estimate, setting the cup within easy reach. Then I curtsied, prepared to flee like a startled rabbit.

The floor jerked up and smacked me. I laid there, stunned, trying to figure out what had happened. The cheek pressed to the warm wood of the study floor hurt from the impact, but the worst of the pain was in the other cheek.

It wasn't the floor that had hit me, I realized, but the duchess.

"I'm sorry, my lady," I said, though I didn't know what I was apologizing for.

"Get up," she said. Calm. Almost kind.

I shuddered. A calm duchess was a dangerous duchess.

That was incentive enough to fight the reeling dizziness and scramble to my feet. I swayed, little bursts of light dancing across my vision. So I didn't see the duchess's next blow. She backhanded the same cheek as before. The settings on her numerous rings cut me, adding another flavor of pain for me to suffer. I hit the floor and stayed there.

The fairy hissed.

"Stop this," he snarled.

The duchess ignored him, planting the sharply pointed toe of her elegant boot in my gut. I curled in on myself, gagging around the desperate need for air. The duchess's next kick struck my spine and I cried out.

I don't know how long it went on like that. The fairy cursed, his wings beating with such fury the air buzzed. The duchess beat me with something—not her infamous riding crop, but something long and hard—or kicked me with booted feet. She kicked my nose. Blood filled my mouth and sprayed the floor. A stray thought rattled through my head. I was going to have to figure out how to remove bloodstains from the rug.

"Enough!"

I wasn't sure if the voice was the fairy's or the duchess's. It didn't matter. The blows stopped, but the pain remained, throbbing deep.

"I will grant you one wish," the fairy said. His voice came from a very long ways away, and I wondered if perhaps he'd found a way to break free of his prison. "In exchange, you must promise to never harm this girl again."

I didn't hear the duchess's response. The lurking oblivion rose up to swallow me whole, and I embraced it with every fiber of my being.

I came to slowly. My body ached, and at first I attributed it to sleeping on the floor. I frowned. Why was I sleeping on the floor?

Memory returned in a rush of pain. I started to move away from the puddle of blood and vomit my cheek rested in, but the movement set light to the hot coals burning in my muscles and joints.

I took stock, counting the aches and pains. The blood came mostly from my nose and the cuts on my cheek. Careful prodding at my abdomen revealed a lot of bruises and sore spots, but nothing that might indicate something inside had been damaged. Mostly, I was just bruised.

It could have been worse. I'd seen worse.

"You live."

The voice was small, and sad. The fairy.

I was still in the duchess's study. Fear flooded my mouth with saliva, followed by the hot taste of bile. I swallowed convulsively, but it was too much. The pain, the stink, the fear.

At least I was already turned on my side so I didn't choke when I was sick.

"I wish there was more I could do for you," the fairy said.

He had stopped the duchess before she beat me to death. He had done plenty.

"Wha—" My tongue felt thick and clumsy. I swallowed, grimaced at the acidic burn, cleared my throat, and tried again. "What did she wish for?"

The silence stretched for so long I decided he wasn't going to tell me. Fine. I breathed deeply to push past the pain, mustering up the strength and courage to move. This time, braced and ready for the rush of pain, I managed to get to my hands and knees, and stayed there to wait for the sparkles across my vision to dim.

"She wished for my name," the fairy said.

He seemed to be waiting for a response, so I grunted.

"A fairy's name cannot be earned by wishing for it," he continued. "Instead, she demanded a slow death for her rival."

"And you granted it," I whispered.

"I gave my word."

A wish in exchange for the duchess's promise. It wasn't my fault someone would die. It *wasn't*. But guilt gnawed at me all the same.

"Will she be forced to keep her promise?" I asked.

"She is human. Always, she is free to choose her actions."

Another three slow, deep breaths, and I shifted from my hands and knees to upright. Mostly upright. I remained kneeling and clung to the fancifully carved edge of the fairy's table while the world tipped and tilted.

"What happens if she breaks her promise?" I asked.

The fairy stared at me. This close, I could see his eyes were gold. Brighter than the gilding of his iron cage.

"She would be forsworn, the bargain broken."

"The wish, too?" I asked.

"If death has not yet found its target, then yes. Health and life would be restored to the rival."

I started to nod, but stopped when it felt like my head might fall right off my neck. Slowly, lips pursed but unable to bite back a whimper, I pushed myself all the way to my feet.

It wasn't my fault the duchess wished death on someone, but it was within my power to stop it. It shouldn't be too hard, considering.

Not trusting the strength of my legs, I refrained from curt-seying to the fairy. I did manage to drop my chin in something that was almost a bow. It was the best I could do.

Turning, I started for the door, weighing the need to brace myself against having to clean the upholstery before the duchess returned and found bloody hand prints everywhere. I didn't want to think about the mess spread across the hard-wood floor or splattered on the expensive rug.

"Girl."

I stopped, waited, but did not turn. It would take too much effort.

"I have a question and a gift for you."

"I don't need a gift," I said. Even to my own ears, I sounded tired. Worn thin.

"Nevertheless, I will give it to you," he said. Before I could protest again, he clattered his wings. "No. You have suffered greatly because of my refusal to submit, and honor demands I repay you somehow. I cannot grant you a wish unless and until I grant the duchess the three owed for my capture. But I can gift you my name."

Effort be damned. I shuffled around to face the fairy. He watched me, solemn. And, I thought, sad. So sad.

"I mean no offense," I said with all the politeness I could muster, "but I don't want your name. I've heard the stories."

He smiled; a small fleeting thing that failed to lift the shadows gathered in his eyes.

"If I give it to you, *that one* cannot have it."

I wrapped the arm not busy keeping me upright across my stomach and dropped my gaze.

"How do you know I won't give it to her?" I asked. "I would, you know. If it was my life or your name, I would give it to her in a heartbeat."

He tipped his head, a gesture more bird-like than human.

"I don't believe you would," he murmured.

I clenched my hand in a fist. He was wrong.

"Nevertheless, it is mine to give where I wish. Riam," he said, and I winced. "My name is Riam."

If I expected to feel the weight of magic his name bore settle on me like a cloak, I would have been disappointed. There was no more magic in it than being offered the name of a new friend. Although friendship, I thought, carried a weight of its own.

I did not thank him for his gift, since no matter what he claimed, that was not the intent behind the giving. I was a guardian of sorts. I would not use his name, but I suspected he was right, and I wouldn't give it to anyone else either.

"And your question?" I asked.

"Why do you come back?"

I frowned, confused.

"What do you mean?" I asked.

"You do not live in this place. It is not your home. So why do you come back? Why subject yourself to that creature's abuse?"

I opened my mouth, but closed it without speaking. How to explain? How to make him understand?

"Because I need this job," I said. "I couldn't afford a place to stay without it, or food to eat. Besides, I have nowhere else to go."

"But you can go anywhere."

I smiled, but it was a bitter, twisted thing. It hurt, so I stopped.

"No, I can't."

I made my way to the door one slow, aching step at a time. The fairy did not speak again.

It was well past dark by the time I made it home. It'd taken me a long time to make my way through the city. Partly because I stuck to alleys and narrow back streets to avoid gawp-mouthed stares from strangers, but mostly because I hurt so much that just putting one foot in front of the other was an effort.

I should have stopped at the apothecary on the corner for something to help with the pain, but I didn't want my neighbors to see me, and I didn't have the money for it. My daily wage had been cut, since Grandine had taken one look at me and sent me home.

Home. I stood in the small room I rented above the herbalist's shop, and stared into the darkness. A single candle waited on the nightstand. A clay pitcher with a chipped rim perched precariously on the narrow mantel with a small wood cup and a shallow basin neatly stacked beside it. The bed was narrow—the straw mattress needed re-stuffing and the rope frame sagged. The wardrobe was squat and narrow, just big enough to hang three dresses. If I were taller, the hems would have laid crumpled on the wardrobe's floor.

The room was tiny, unadorned, and always smelled of astringent herbs or incense smoke, but it was clean. It was a roof over my head, and the herbalist let me use the small stove in her workroom to cook, as long as I was careful not to disturb her things. It had always been enough for me.

I leaned my bruised back against the door, closed my eyes, and slid to the floor.

But you can go anywhere, the fairy's voice whispered.

Could I? I didn't have much money. Didn't have any real skills beyond wielding a mop and dustpan. I couldn't just pack up my belongings—meager though they were—and leave. Where would I go? What would I do? I grew up in the city. My life was here.

For the first time in a long time, I wished that weren't true. I wished, desperately, hopelessly, for the courage to walk out the city gates and just keep going. I could follow whatever road I wished, or carve a path of my own. I could—

What? What could I do? Offer to clean the houses of farmers in exchange for food?

I buried my face in my hands, but did not cry. I didn't have tears to spend on mourning what I could never have.

My mother once told me people fear change, and that fear grows greater with each passing year. The old grandma fears the small changes more than a warrior fears going into battle against overwhelming odds.

"Change isn't always bad," Mother said. "But it *is* hard."

I hadn't understood what she meant. Not then, but I was beginning to. Why did I continue working for a woman who abused her servants on a regular basis? Who trapped a fairy in a gilded iron cage, and used my pain to force him to grant a wish he did not want to give?

Because I was scared. More scared of what might happen if I left the duchess's employ than of the duchess herself.

I stewed about it for the next several days, while I kept my head down and finished my work as quickly as possible. I traded rooms with another maid so I wouldn't have to go near the study. I was being a coward, I knew it, but I couldn't stand the idea of facing the fairy. Riam. I could hardly believe he'd given me, *me*, his name.

To the shock of the rest of the staff, the duchess was cheerful and almost kind. She returned from a visit to the royal palace all but humming. The crown prince, it seemed, had fallen ill.

"And no matter what the court physicians do, they won't be able to cure him," she said, and laughed.

Laughed.

I knew then, the target of her wish. Knew I could stop it. I could save the prince. All I had to do was give up the shield of fear I hid behind.

The perfect opportunity presented itself two days later. It had stormed that morning, leaving the city sopping with mud. Mud the servants tracked through the back halls, and the duchess's guests tracked in through the front door. I spent all morning and most of the afternoon mopping up filthy footprints, and the water in my bucket showed it.

I had just finished cleaning the last of the footprints in the grand foyer when the duchess came striding through the front door, marring the pristine floors. I shrank away from her, head ducked low as I curtsied a greeting with all the other lowly servants waiting to attend her. If she had been alone, I would have quietly crept off to find a corner to hide in. But she wasn't alone. A lord stepped inside behind her. Grand and regal, he moved with a grace born of unmatched confidence and the assurance that all men stood beneath him.

I didn't give myself time to think about what I was about to do. If I did, I would talk myself out of it, and this needed to happen. A life hung on my paltry courage, which was more terrifying than stumbling into the duchess's path and sloshing muddy water on her impeccable sharp-toed boots.

A collective gasp echoed from the arched ceiling and bounced amongst the frescoes. I froze, staring aghast at what I'd done. I was mid-apology when the duchess whipped her riding crop across my face. My still aching cheek exploded with pain, and I dropped to the floor with a whimper. I curled into a ball, hands over my head, and did the only thing I could.

"I'm sorry, I'm sorry, please, my lady," I begged. "Please don't hurt me."

Her boot heel struck the tile with a sound like mountains breaking, backed by her low, growling hiss.

"Harrietta."

The soft, masculine voice cut through the rising tension like sun through rainclouds. I peeked beneath my elbow and saw the grand lord rest a gloved hand on the duchess's shoulder. She stilled at the touch. After a second—a minute, an eternity —she stepped back and shook out her skirts, trying to hide her fluster.

"You," the lord said to me, not unkindly. "Clean your lady's boots, then begone."

"Yes, my lord."

I scrambled to my knees and used my own apron to polish away the muck.

"There, see? No harm done," the lord said.

The duchess grumbled, but she was too pleased by his attentiveness to protest.

I was glad for the excuse to keep my head bowed. I didn't want the duchess to see my face. Didn't want her to remember me, and the promise she'd made.

Because as soon as she did, she was going to kill me.

"Was it you?!"

The scream rang through the hallways. It was followed by the familiar crack of a riding crop striking flesh, and a whimper of pain.

"Was it you?" the duchess screamed.

Every nerve in my body jangled with the urge to run. That furious scream was nowhere near me, and I wanted it to stay that way. My heart leapt in my chest like a wild thing, throwing itself against my ribcage hard enough to hurt.

She knew, it chanted, desperate with fear. *She knew, she knew, she knew.*

I did not run. Instead, I turned back to the concealed entrance of the servants' passage and quietly set my supplies inside. Then I crept down the hallway. *Toward* the sounds of shattering glass, breaking wood, and the muffled cries of a woman in pain.

Reaching the corner, I pressed my back to the wall, closed my eyes and forced my lungs to fill.

Carefully, so carefully, I eased forward and peered into the grand foyer. A maid lay on the blood-splattered floor, so still I wasn't sure she was conscious. The duchess stood on the far side of the massive room. She jerked a vase from its plinth and hurled it against the wall, barely missing the head of a terrified footman.

The maid, I noticed with sick dread, had brown hair only a shade or two lighter than my own.

Oh, yes. The duchess knew. Her unthinking brutality had worked against her. She broke her promise to the fairy. The wish was negated. Her rival was no longer destined to die a slow death. The only reason it wasn't me lying on the marble floor in a puddle of blood was the duchess's inability to see and recognize servants as individuals.

A fork in the path of my life loomed before me. I could leave. Leave the home I'd made for myself, the city I'd grown up in, the kingdom my family had belonged to for as long as anyone could remember. Or I could remain and let the duchess kill me.

Hands clenched into fists, I slid away from the grand foyer and the continued sounds of violence. I regretted leaving the other maid behind, but there was nothing I could do for her. If I went out there, I would be offering myself to Death.

No, I couldn't help my fellow maid, but there was someone else I could save.

The duchess's study was in shambles. Books had been torn from their shelves and flung across the room. The contents of the desk laid scattered on the floor, the broken inkwell creating a creeping pool that reminded me of the maid's blood. Anything breakable had been broken, including the duchess's precious decanter of brandy. The table that had once stood in the center of it all had been upended, the fairy's cage gone.

Palms slick with terrified sweat, I hurried into the room looking for the fairy. It didn't take me long to find him. His cage lay on its side on the floor partially buried by the mess. The ornate bars were bent, the swing detached from its hook, leaving no safe place for the fairy.

He lay with his swing. His wings were grey as ash, his skin colorless except for the black splotches where it came in direct contact with the iron bars.

"Riam," I whispered, grief threatening to smother me.

He stirred at the sound of his name. I dropped to my knees, ignoring the bits of debris that dug into me.

"Sweet girl," he murmured, his voice so weak I had to press my nose to the bars of his cage to hear him. "It was you, wasn't it? You broke the wish."

"I slopped mud on her boots and she struck me. She strikes

anyone who displeases her. It's a habit so deeply ingrained, I don't think she could have stayed her hand even if she realized who she was hitting."

"She didn't know?"

I shrugged. "One maid is much the same as another to her. She would have hit me eventually."

I just made sure she did it in time to save the prince's life.

"Brave girl," Riam said, and smiled before he closed his eyes again.

"Yes, well. I'm about to be very cowardly." It was a struggle for him to open his eyes again, but he managed it, and looked a question at me. "I'm running away. I'm leaving the city entirely. Probably the kingdom, too. I came to free you."

"Free me," he whispered.

"Let's get you out of there," I said.

"No," he said. "You should go. Now. Before she catches you here. It is too late for me."

I ignored him. I struggled with the little sliding door. With the bars bent as they were, it didn't want to move. I finally hunted for and found the duchess's knife-like letter opener and used it to pry the cage open.

A distant door slammed and I jumped. As carefully as I could, I scooped Riam onto my palm. With him cupped in both hands, and both hands held close to my chest, I made my escape from the study. From the duchess's mansion. From my gilded cage built of habit and fear.

I strode out of the city and into the unknown without a single glance back.

Following the road would have been faster. I didn't want to make it easy for the duchess to find me, so I trudged across muddy fields to the distant forest. I walked until the sun began to set and the darkening shadows made further travel too dangerous. I found shelter in the hollow beneath a fallen tree and sank wearily to the ground.

"Riam?"

I lowered my hands to my lap to check on him, but he didn't stir. In the rapid approach of night, I couldn't see his wings at all, and I tried not to consider where the fine powder coating my fingers had come from.

"Riam?" I said, my voice shaking.

He was so still. I didn't know what else to do but keep him warm, so that's what I did. I held him close and tried hard not to hear his last words to me.

It wasn't too late. It wasn't. We had made it. We *would* make it. I'd carry him far away from the city and the duchess and return him to the wild woods where he belonged.

"You're free, Riam," I whispered. "You're free."

We both were.

By morning, nothing remained of the fairy but the white dust of his wings staining my hands.

With no remains to offer back to the forest, I buried my fingers in the rich loam and made a silent promise. Never again would I allow myself to be caged by fear. I would live, and I would find happiness in my freedom.

It was a long time before I found the courage to stand and begin walking. Taking that first step was like trying to lift a boulder. Impossible. But I managed it. The second wasn't as hard, and the third easier still. With each steady step, I moved forward to embrace whatever my future held in store.

J. MILLIGAN (Blue Quill Chapter) is striving to make her debut in traditional publishing, so alas, no book accolades for her. She's a hungering void when it comes to all things fantasy, and she has a special love for the ridiculous, which at least partially explains her fondness for Japanese anime. She currently lives in her childhood home with her old blind dog and her elderly parents. She takes particular joy in feeding them (dog included) delectable meals whipped up by her kitchen wizardry. Join J. on her journey to publication by following her on Twitter at @writingdemons.

Familial Ties

Sarah Murtagh

E scaping an abusive mother was a nightmare. Leaving my younger sister behind was even worse.

Two years later, gentle rain splattered the windows of my apartment as I listened to my sister three thousand miles away. Years of safety and therapy had cooled my anxiety, but sudden sounds could still yank me into a panic. Too-loud heels or a door slammed by the wind would set my heart battering against my rib cage.

Asha still lived with that, but instead of moments, it was every day.

"I'm sorry for calling you like this." Her voice trembled, and I had to raise the volume of my phone to hear her. It was storming back east too. Inside Asha's car, the torrent of rain upon glass echoed with thunder, the sounds reverberating in her tiny Toyota.

"Don't apologize."

"I shouldn't have been angry at you for leaving."

"I get it," I told her. "Believe me, I do."

"I don't know how much longer I can take this. I finally

finished college, but now that I'm trying to find a job, she's so much worse."

This time it didn't take an unexpected sound to rush my heartbeat. I knew well enough that even a calm day with my mother was still a bad one. Even thinking about it could raise my blood pressure.

"I used to think I could handle it." Asha raised her voice over the storm. "I used to think I could help her, or I thought maybe I owed her. But I need to get out. And all of my friends' parents know her. I can't go to them. I don't know what to do."

Each day, I did my best not let my mind live in the past or remember being trapped back there and terrified. Living in a house like that, unease never fully left, not really. My body reacted quicker than my mind, searching for signs of danger. Even when I'd finally escaped, what I thought might be elation morphed into its own kind of prison—one I was still dealing with. How could I free myself when my body was free but my mind wasn't?

My mother's taunts echoed in my head at every mistake—a spilled cup, a missed bus. I couldn't go a day without her phantom pressing into every crevice of my newfound freedom.

It didn't feel like winning a race, leaving that sort of house. It felt like escaping into the woods, where a hunter might be waiting to shoot me down. The first few months, I still felt like I was suffocating, with only moments of breath.

Time, therapy, safety, and support became more valuable to me than anything.

Those moments when I felt it, truly felt that I was out—having the freedom to enjoy peace, to have my own space, my own ability to choose, my own nights alone, no longer fearing, no longer dreading—it was a slow release of relief.

It got easier, in the way that one day I walked down the street and felt something in my chest. It startled me. It was unfamiliar. After moments of confusion, I realized it was happiness. Relief and joy without fear, bright and unadulterated.

I didn't know I could feel something like that.

"I don't know what to do," Asha repeated. She sounded close to breaking.

In that moment, nothing could have stopped me. If the call had been disconnected or if she'd changed her mind and hung up, it wouldn't have mattered. I would have found a way to reach her.

When I first left, I couldn't have helped her on my own. But now I could. If my leaving first was to have any greater meaning, it would be that I had gained strength to help her too.

Whatever would have freed me from that place, I would have been grateful. It turned out to be a friend with a kind heart, a couch for me to sleep on, and some extra money to help me until I could pay my own way.

Now, two years later, I could do that for my sister.

"Hey . . . ," I said, trying to speak loud enough to be heard over the rain, but thunder clapped in my ear. I closed my eyes as I breathed carefully, trying to calm my nerves and racing heart. It sounded like a threat, like a slap to a wall that preceded something worse. "I will get you out. I will help you."

"You will? Seriously?"

"Yeah."

As I said it, regret pierced me. I should have been the one to reach out. But I couldn't turn back the clock.

"Thank you. Really."

"Give me maybe two months. Then I'll fly you out here." I calculated my expenses in my head—how much I could save, the cost of a flight, and how much I might need to support her while she found a job. Two months sounded reasonable. Any amount of time was too long, but it was what I could do. "In the meantime, can you hold out? Prepare what you can?"

"Yes. God, if I know I'm leaving, everything will be easier to deal with."

Two months. Things would be tight, and I'd need to tell my friends I couldn't go on the trip we'd planned. But that didn't matter if it meant getting my sister safe. There was no question.

Nothing was more precious than a life lived in safety, a life beginning to heal, a life beginning to truly feel like life.

SARAH MURTAGH (Salt City Genre Writers) is a writer with a fierce love of mythology, history, and cats. Her stories explore the darker aspects of life, often blended with gods and dark magic, but she promises she's friendly—just don't interrupt her when she's reading. Originally from Maryland, she now lives in Salt Lake City, Utah where she is a proud member of the League of Utah Writers. When she's not writing, or nose-deep in research and reporting as a Data Analyst, she spends time with her black cat and twin sister. You can find her on Twitter @sarahandstories.

Deprogrammed

Johnny Worthen

"Is she awake?"

"Oh, yeah."

"Pissed off?"

"I'd so say."

"Violent?"

"Not yet, but I wouldn't put it past her."

Rick took in the information while unloading sacks of Mexican take-out on the kitchen counter.

"Is there any... thing you want to tell me?" asked Shaun.

"Like is there a manhunt out for us? No. Nothing on the news. Clean grab."

"She's not what I expected," Shaun said.

"How so?"

"She seems, I don't know. Normal."

"Because she wasn't in robes? Bald or tattooed? Not chanting mantras or spells? Don't believe it. She's not normal. She's been trained to appear that way. I know, I helped write that training."

Shaun took in the information standing at near attention, awaiting orders.

Rick had hired Shaun—last name unknown—from a site on the Dark Web that claimed black-ops connections. The man said he'd been in the military, but since names were out, resumes were too. He looked like he had been—big beefy arms that said pull-ups for breakfast, a sleek bald scalp of an alpha male. He knew how to handle a gun, but his tattoos spoke of prison. Rick wasn't sure of his pedigree. Only four days into the project and he was already losing his nerve.

"If you want to back out, I can do without you now," Rick said.

"Nah, nah, I'm good."

"Then let's get this started then. Bring her out."

Shaun pulled a ski mask out of his pocket and looked at it.

"Your call," said Rick.

"She'll thank us later?"

"Absolutely."

He dropped the mask on a barstool and headed upstairs.

Rick watched him go, admiring after he'd disappeared down a hallway the pine bannisters and luxury ceiling of the cabin. Blond knotty wood, a scent of sap underlying the smell of hot spices coming from the bags. This place couldn't have been cheap. Seven thousand square feet, eight bedrooms, three family rooms, five car garage, hot tub, play room, more bathrooms than he'd been able to count, and two full kitchens. It would be a great corporate retreat, but it was a family summer house up in the mountains, by a private lake. The Rogers were as rich as they were big. Six kids. Deidre the middle of the three girls. Nineteen years old. The black sheep. His patient.

Rick set the table in the little breakfast nook of the kitchen rather than use any of the formal ones. An intimate first encounter, a counterpoint to the pain to come, a promise for the end of the treatments.

He'd expected to hear a string of profanities from Deidre

Rogers as Shaun marched her down the stairs in chains. She'd been vocal enough in the bathroom and parking lot when they'd snatched her. Quick to kick and scream in the car trunk, only shutting up after he'd given her the shot. Even then, beneath the tape, she'd gone under with a half-spoken expletive on her lips.

"Miss Rogers." Rick tipped his chin in welcome.

"Fuck you," she said.

"Are you hungry?" he asked her.

"I can tell that it's nighttime, but what day of night?"

"Does it matter?"

"Yes. If it's Sunday, I haven't eaten in a day. Monday two. Tuesday three days. See how it goes?"

"It's Monday night."

"Then yeah, I'm hungry."

"Sit down."

Shaun helped her to the chair. The restraints were the prison kind, ankles and wrists. Shaun released her hands but gave her a long meaningful look as he did.

She rolled her eyes at him before peeling the lid off the takeout tray set in front of her. "Salad?"

"You don't like salad?" said Rick. Shaun sat down.

"I love salad, but not when I haven't eaten in days."

Rick felt a blush on his cheeks but swallowed it back. "So you would like mine?" He showed her the chili verde stuffed burrito he had.

"That looks like it'll stick on the ribs. Yes, I want it."

"It's meat."

"There's meat on this salad."

"You can't pick it out so easily as the salad. You'll have to eat some."

"I'll manage."

He smiled. "You need to ask for it."

She looked at him, looked hard. She studying him.

"Please can I have some food so I don't die?" she said not taking her eyes off him.

He passed the tray to Shaun who exchanged it for the salad and delivered that back. His own burrito lay untouched.

She fell onto the food so aggressively that she broke her plastic fork.

"There's some real silverware in the top left drawer of the island," she said and pointed. When no one got up to fetch it, she tried to, but Shaun pushed her down.

"Big man," she said and stabbed at her food with a plastic knife.

Rick poked at the salad pretending everything was going to plan. He let everyone eat for a while and then spoke. "Aren't you curious what this is all about?"

"I know what this is all about," she said.

"If you're thinking we kidnapped you for a ransom—"

"I know what this is all about," she said again. "I figured it out when I woke up. My parents sent you. Why else would you be in their house?"

"Maybe we thought this was a good place to hide. The last place anyone would look for you."

At this she chewed and smiled.

"How's the pork?" he asked.

She flipped him the finger.

"You're a vegetarian?" said Shaun.

Rick gave him a look. He wasn't supposed to say a goddam word.

She nodded.

"Is everyone at your cult vegetarians?"

She nodded again. "And you are?"

"I'm Rick. The large man there is my associate."

"Shaun."

"Glad to meet you Shaun. I'm Clara."

"What?" Shaun looked at Rick, finally seeing the hard stare. "I thought you were Deidre ?" he said in retreat.

"Nope. Clara Earthbright. Looking for a Deidre ? Oops. You got the wrong girl, guys. Sorry. Can you drop me off at the bus station? There's one in Sanders Creek on Fifth. That's only like eight miles down the road."

"Why did you change your name?" said Rick.

"Kicks."

"He makes you do that," said Rick. "It's to remove you from your old life—your family, friends, connections. It's meant to isolate you from your support group. It's a way to control you. I've seen it before."

"Yeah, where? Bootcamp?"

"I was a member of COTNE," said Rick, smoothly, calmly. Confidently. "Before your time, but I was. Back when Rasul wasn't Rasul, but just old Jamie, Jamie Galat, eccentric tycoon with a bunch of crystals and an emerging case of raging narcissism."

"Can I get something to drink?" she asked. "I'm sure there's some KoolAid around here somewhere. Look in the pantry."

"How long has it been since you were last here?" asked Rick.

"It's been a while. Four years."

"You left home at fifteen."

"I did indeed. Shaun, would you mind? Water. Milk. Something."

He looked at Rick who nodded, got up and went to the kitchen.

She slid her finger over the tray and licked it clean. Shaun arrived with a glass of water, put it down, picked up her debris and took it away. The plastic knife was not among it.

"Here's how it's going to be," said Rick. "This isn't going to be quick. This isn't going to be easy. In fact, I think it'll probably be the hardest thing you've ever done. I'm going to bring you back. I'm going to free you from COTNE and Rasul and return you to the real world."

"How much are you getting paid?"

"This is just a greeting," he said gesturing to the table like it was a grand feast. "We won't meet like this again, not until you've made real progress. You will sleep in a room we've prepared for you in the basement. You'll receive bread and water and be in the dark some time. Occasionaly we will visit, I will show you things, data, pictures, films. I'll share stories of other survivors like me, like you will be. The setting and content of our visits will be contingent on your cooperation."

"I'm sold. I give up. I've seen the light. I hereby three times deny Rasul and the Celebrants of the New Eon. They are false and I was used. I am better now. I repent. Will you be my husband?"

"It's for your own good. You don't think so now, but we are freeing you."

"From what?"

"From evil."

"Oh, that."

Rick didn't like her attitude. It was too flippant. The other two clients he'd had weren't this self-possessed. They were more afraid, stricter with the cult's alignment. That Clara— Deidre , he reminded himself, had already spoken denunciation of Rasul, albeit sarcastically and with a flourish, was a new twist to this. He'd expected a rigidity, one that could shatter. This suggested plasticity, pliable but ultimately more unyielding.

Rick was a deprogrammer. It was an occupation once much in the news, but now only a curiosity. He had a special set of skills that worked in the shady outskirts of the social, spiritual, and legal worlds. There was no school to go to for it, no letters to put after his name, nowhere to openly trade his services. Still, he'd found a niche and had lately been in demand.

"Are you done eating?" asked Rick.

"Got any cake?"

"No. Would you like some salad?"

"Since you're not having it, sure." She reached across the table for it, but Shaun grabbed her wrist halfway. "Why so jumpy? Afraid a little gal like me will getcha'?"

He bent her hand back and removed the plastic knife from it.

"Maybe we should put you away for now," said Rick, "bring you back when you're in a better frame of mind."

"No, I'm good. Let's talk, Nestor." She smirked when he betrayed his surprise.

"Fork?" she asked pointing to his.

He shook his head.

She ate with her fingers.

"How do you know that name? I've been out of COTNE for five years."

She held a finger up for him to wait while she chewed.

"I guess I left an impression," said Rick leaning back in his chair, happy he'd had a big lunch.

"You didn't," she said. "We figured out who you were after you took Annebelle and Drake."

"So the great Rasul remembers me. I'm flattered."

"He said you were a disappointment."

"I bet he did."

"If he could only see you now." She rattled the chains for effect.

"There are chains young lady and there are chains."

"Really? Oh wow—"

Shaun's slap caught her across the chin, spinning her head.

"No!" Rick had blurted it out for Shaun, but before the sound was out he realized his mistake. It would show a lack of discipline on their parts, question his authority. He turned it quickly. "No. Deidre . That kind of attitude is not helpful."

Slowly she pulled her chin off her shoulder, turned to face Shaun, unblinkingly and firm, and then she settled on Rick. Looking him straight in the eye, she spat bloody lettuce into his face.

Shaun raised his hand again making her flinch.

"No," said Rick and wiped his face with a paper napkin. "I don't think we need any more of that, do you?" he said.

She put a napkin to her bloody lip.

"Rasul had years to scramble your brain, Deidre. Unscrambling it will take some effort."

"Rasul never hit me."

"No. His violence was much more subtle. Less…. honest, shall we say?"

"Let's not." She flinched when she said it, expecting Shaun to hit her again.

Rick prayed he wouldn't. He hadn't told him to. He wondered why he'd done it, then remembered that he'd mentioned that a slap during the deprogramming was part of the routine, it did wonders in fact. But it had to be done at the right time and in the right way and it had to be done by the deprogrammer. Everything depended on the patient transferring affection to him, not to the hired help. It had to be him that communicated, that explained, counseled, cajoled, sympathized, hurt, and then nurtured back into form. Shaun had set his work back a week at least. He was a liability now. He'd need to get rid of Shaun.

"Let's begin again," said Rick. "We'll all mind our manners."

She rattled her chains for a reply.

Rick signaled Shaun to take off her ankle cuffs. When it was done, he said, "Good. Now, let's have a nice chat and get a sense of where we'll be tomorrow."

"I'll be home tomorrow," said Clara.

"You are home," said Rick. "Or is that not what you meant?"

"It's great to be kidnapped to a familiar place, but no. This house, this is part of your world, is not mine anymore."

"And now your home is the commune?"

"You know it's more than that."

"I know nothing."

"I'll let that one alone," she said and glanced at Shaun who stared blankly back at her.

"This is a nice place. Beautiful house," said Rick. "Ten foot windows, view of mountains and lake. You're very lucky to have all this."

She looked out into darkness, but didn't reply.

"Your family loves you very much."

Still nothing.

"It's an irony. Your parents and their parents worked so hard for this—for you. They suffered and scrimped and saved to get ahead in life, to make something for their kids, so you'd have it easier than they did. In the end, it was just too easy for you, so soft for you that it made you susceptible to Rasul and COTNE. That kind of cancer can only find purchase in soft tissue."

"Why'd you leave?"

"I saw through it. I figured out the con."

"Go on."

It was a juncture, precursor microcosm of the whole process. A question about his involvement, his knowledge. A challenge to be sure, but also a teaching moment. He let it hang thinking he should end the interview now, leave it suspended, returning to it in a week, as a moment of candor. That's what the books had suggested, but he followed his gut and continued, still thinking of making up for Shaun's missteps.

"It's false," he said. "It's not the real world. It's a pretend paradise. While Rasul is selling flower child communism bunk inside, COTNE Incorporated is out in the real world making bank on the labor of their gullible cultists. It's a big money company, while you eat rice."

"I like rice."

"You liked that burrito too."

"I see your point. It was better than the salad. That tasted like blood."

She pulled back in her chair, distancing herself from Shaun who sat still as a board, his eyes fixed emotionlessly on her. He reminded Rick of a machine. A menace machine, programmed and now operating at peak efficiency. Maybe he could use it. He'd not gone so physical before, but then again, he'd never had anyone as blithe as Deidre before.

"It's about efficiency," he said. "No one ever got rich working for themselves."

She nodded in agreement.

"Wealth comes from exploitation."

"That's what Rasul teaches."

"And he should know."

"He made his money in real estate."

"How does he make it now?"

She shrugged. "He doesn't need to."

"But he is making money and you know how he's doing. He's richer now than he's ever been."

"The Celebrants of the New Eon are a community. We pool our resources."

"That's one way to say it, right out of the brochures, but there's a scam happening and you're part of it. You know how we found you?"

She shook her head, scooted a little farther away from Shaun.

"We found one of your sculptures in a Jackson Hole gallery.

It was going for twelve thousand dollars. How much of that will you see?"

She shrugged. Her eyes darted around, no longer meeting his. Fixing on Shaun for a moment, the window the next, the table, her hands. A good sign.

"The gallery will take fifty percent, which leaves you exactly... nothing. Am I right? It all goes to the collective?"

"It's how it should be."

"I'm told your work is well received. You've won some awards for it, did you know that? Best of show at the Evanston Art Walk last year."

"I didn't know that."

"Cash prize of a thousand dollars and the piece sold for twenty," he said. "And yet when we picked you up, you had eleven dollars and a COTNE business Visa in your pocket."

"Before I joined the Celebrants of the New Eon my family had arranged my entire life," she said.

"Rebellion was your motive then?"

"No... well, maybe."

"That's interesting. I call that progress."

"The point I wanted to make was about my ancestors like you were talking about. My parents followed their parents. The ancestor's vision. True to form, they set it all up. Had a place for me and everything."

"A wonderful life ahead of you. And it's not too late to rejoin it."

"Tradition," she said, "is just peer pressure from dead people."

"That's a new one."

"I didn't want that world."

"Were they forcing you?"

"Yes."

"Bullshit."

"Coercion, disappointment, emotional blackmail. Nothing

as direct as Shaun's two brain-cell slap, but effective all the way. As long as I stayed in that family, I was subject to their pressure. I was in a cage."

"And to flee that you flew into a worse one."

"I flew to freedom."

"No you didn't. You have more restraints on you now than ever."

"I chose them."

"No. No you didn't. Rasul did. He takes your labor and limits who you can see. Your family is on the list right? You're not allowed to have anything to do with them."

"Because they're unhealthy for me."

"Because they're in the best position to save you."

"They didn't like my art," she said. "Dad said it was stupid, Mom worried about my anti-religious theme. It was getting in the way of my marriage."

"You were engaged?"

"No. But they were planning on it. I was told that once I got over my selfish phase, I'd surely land a husband. The selfish phase was me creating art, hanging out with people they didn't like."

"So it's religion and not politics that motivates you?"

"They're pretty related when you believe in what you're doing."

"You didn't like the faith of your fathers?"

"I don't even like that hymn."

"More peer pressure from dead people? That's why you left?"

"Family? Or church? Or society as a—you know what? It's all the same thing. The answer is yes to all that, but that doesn't say much. I'd say it was all their hypocrisy and villainy."

"Those words don't say much more."

"How much is Rasul worth?" she asked.

"I have no idea."

"Yes you do. You have some idea."

Shaun twitched his head down the hallway. "You hear that?"

Rick shook his head. He kept his eyes on Clara—Deidre, who looked anywhere but at his.

"I'll go check." Shaun stood up heavily as if lifting his torso off the chair was a workout and went toward the back of the house.

"Best estimate is COTNE has around twenty million dollars," Rick said.

"Hypocrisy incorporated is sitting on over a hundred billion."

"How's that villainy?"

"They're sitting on it."

"Wealth distribution. Revolution. I can see the attraction. Wrong and misguided but understandable in one so young. Still, I'd think you'd be interested in the talk of enlightenment."

"I got some of that."

"And free love?"

"Cheaper than what was on offer," she said. "That's for sure."

"You call yourself a communist?"

"Socialist."

"Socialism is responsible for how many deaths?"

"A fraction of what capitalism is," she said.

"Capitalism is the worst system in the world, except for all the others," he said.

"Please…"

"What's wrong with capitalism? Look what it can do?" He waved his arms around the kitchen then felt stupid, as if a stainless steel fridge was some kind of monument.

"You measured my worth by what my art sold for. That's capitalism. Rasul values me by me, expressed by my art."

"So he can sell it. You're his slave. All you do is for him."

"I'm no one's slave. I'm a part of something. At the commune, we all share. We work together. Cooperate and don't compete. Our excesses go to the betterment of others. We are content."

"You speak for everyone?"

"Okay. Me. I am whole. I want for nothing and the things I used to want—the things you're told to want, I don't anymore. I have everything I need. I live in peace. I am content."

"Stockholm syndrome. He's taken your ambition. Your drive."

"Because I don't want to compete? Because I want to define myself by these instead of those standards I've fallen in love with my abuser? That's pretty messed up, Nestor."

"Call me Rick, Deidre ."

"Call me Clara, Nestor."

Rick shook his head. If Shaun had been there, he'd have sent her to the garage at that. She was getting too many digs in, too effectively using jargon and clichéd deflections.

"You work for Rasul."

"I work for the Celebrants."

"Same thing. I however, work for myself."

"The hell you do. You're hired out to my family but you work for a bank. A landlord. A bad hairdresser who can't deal with split ends."

"I can work for whomever I want. I go wherever I want. Talk to whomever I want. I benefit from my work."

"And?"

"See the difference?"

"No."

"You're forbidden to see your parents."

"You're forbidden to see Rasul."

"I don't want to."

"See the difference?"

He snorted. She was feisty. It would take time, dark time, hungry time, maybe cold or over-hot times but she'd break.

"I left because it was so limiting."

"And you weren't getting all you could out of your labor."

"All I *should*," he corrected her.

She shrugged and glanced down the hall to where Shaun had disappeared.

"He'll come after you," Rick said. "He won't let you leave. He'll treat you as an escaped prisoner."

She responded that with a surprised smile.

"What?"

"Sounds familiar." Smile still in place.

"Oh it's true," he said. "Rasul will send agents—"

"Did you really hate COTNE that much?" she said.

"Hate is a strong word. I wasn't free. Now I'm free and I'm using my freedom to free others."

"You kidnapped me at the mall."

"So?"

"Know what I was doing there?"

"Recruiting."

"Tomato tomoto."

She thought she'd made some kind of point, but he didn't get it. He wished he had, because now she looked straight at him with hard confident eyes.

He said "The world—" but the words were ripped out of his mouth in a burst of light and sound that bashed the side of his skull like a board, knocking him to the floor.

He thought he heard gunshots, screams, shattering glass, breaking doors, but he couldn't be sure, all was drowned in ringing pain.

He rolled to his right and hit his head on a table leg, cutting his forehead above his right brow. He breathed in acrid smoke that burned his eyes and throat. He coughed and sputtered, vomited bile that splattered the backs of his hands.

The world was ringing and smoke. Gray light that hurt to see.

He crawled forward feeling his way with his hands, eyes clenched, trailing blood from his brow, feeling it with his knees as he moved.

Another explosion, deafening and close, a light he saw through this eyelids.

He fell flat and waited, still as death for a long long moment, until he felt a gust of wind chill his besweated back. He felt forward and found a wall, lifted himself to it, leaned and waited. All the while he fought with his befuddled mind, reaching for ideas, identities, definitions, chasing his thoughts, unable to remember where he was or what he was doing. For the longest time all was scrambled, broken, erased, wiped— then slowly, he remembered the mountain cabin, the job. The Rogers girls.

The breeze blew steady and he chanced to open his eyes.

The gas was gone, for he'd realized it had was tear gas that had flooded the room after a flash-bang grenade had dazed him.

He blinked away the tears, blood from of his right eye. The big panoramic window was broken. The chairs around the table, all disarrayed. The shackles were kicked to the wall. Shaun was nowhere to be seen, and Clara, of course, was gone.

JOHNNY WORTHEN (Infinite Monkeys, Salt City Genre Writers, The Usual Suspects) is an award-winning, multiple-genre, tie-dye-wearing author, voyager, and damn fine human being! A Utah Writer of the Year, trained in literary criticism and cultural studies, he writes upmarket fiction, long and short, mentors others where he can and teaches writing at the University of Utah.

You can keep up with him at www.johnnyworthen.com where you can join his mailing list and download a free book. What's not to love?

With Local Writers

Each week this column will feature the activities and achievements of the Provo Chapter of the League of Utah Writers.

* *   * *   * *

August 10 to 11 are the dates of the Writer's Roundup to be held in Ogden, under the management of the Blue Quill chapter of the League of Utah Writers. Mrs. Florence Glines is president of the group and will be in charge of arrangements. She will be assisted by LaRene King Bleecker, vice president, and Mrs. Merrill Oyler, secretary-treasurer.

Committees are working overtime to make the Round-Up one of the biggest and best ever held in the state. Frank C. Robertson, state league president is contacting speakers from all parts of the state. There will be several outstanding writers from various parts of the United States in attendance as speakers and round-table discussers, as some of them prefer to be called. It's a funny thing that people who can write well are usually not good public speakers. I mean, not fluent, and not at ease speaking before audiences. This is perhaps natural. A writer doesn't have time to talk. He makes his fingers and the typewriter keys express his brilliant ideas. But whether they are considered orators or not, it's the best contact a writer can get—association with other writers who have made good. I understand that one of the guest "round-table-discussers" is to be Sam Taylor, a native of Provo, who is really going to town.

People who want to learn the writing game, surely should be in attendance at the convention. Besides the speakers and the discussions, there will be market tips, hints on seasonal material, "how I broke in" pep talks and everything. Then of course there are the dinners. And the poet's breakfast. This is one of the outstanding events of any roundup. There are always more reservations for this event than any other. Don't we just love to talk about our children! Brain children best of all.

So remember the date and keep it open. Contact members of the Provo Chapter League of Utah Writers for detailed information as to registration fees and transportation. Everyone is invited to attend. Anyone interested in writers, or in writing—or just in the fun of it, are welcome.

One of the highlights of the convention will be the installation of the new South-East chapter, of Price-Helper and vicinities. Initiations are always fun. Writers, has it occurred to you that your own organization may be able to help you solve your problems

Mrs. Susie Jepperson was guest of honor at a pleasant party given by Mrs. Alta Jolley at her home Wednesday afternoon. Mrs. Fern Laudie read a short story, "The Diamond Necklace." The Misses Genevieve and Elizabeth Gordon sang a duet, "The Cabin in the Lane." A delicious luncheon was served the following, Mrs. C. E. Crandall, Mrs. Sarah Prestwich, Mrs. Fern Laudie, Mrs. Bessie Ex-

The Safe Space

Miranda Hughes

A taste of saltwater I had sampled five months ago rests on my tongue, thin as an afterthought, as I exfoliate my lungs with Atlantic air. All around me the sand of the beach is black with chunks of ice the size of children dotting its shore. To my left, a bridge; to my right, grey fog; before me, sunrise; behind me, the moon. Within me, around me, is safety, the first of its kind since it fled into the recesses of my mind so many years ago.

"Breathe in, open your eyes when you are ready."

She is the only voice allowed to speak here, as long as she remains disembodied. I breathe until the air was the smell of a therapist's office and opened my eyes. This room is warm, with minimal stimuli. There is a soft yellow glow of a floor lamp to my right, a door to my left. Behind me, an empty wall, and before me, my therapist. I sit, hunched, hands wrapped together between my knees.

I chose her because she is a trauma specialist. Because she was a warm smile on a website of professional headshots. Because her eyes could translate into the word "empathy."

Because I could afford her services. Because I was tired, so tired, of mucking my own fear after almost twenty years.

"How was that?"

She called the technique Safe Space something. In minutes she helped me break open a new room in my brain, a place untouched and unmarred by the experiences of the last couple of decades and filled it with an abundance of magic and pure safety. I relay this to her.

"Are you ready to do the EMDR?"

"Let's find a memory to focus on."

"You feel ready to focus on that one today?"

It is the memory I need to focus on today. Its trauma is a monument that other thoughts pass every day, every night, sometimes going right past, sometimes stopping to dwell. It is the monument of a particular trauma's dictatorship over this wrinkled grey matter that color and knowledge pass through. It is time I begin breaking it down. This is relayed to my therapist. We congregate around the monument.

"I want you to recall something specific about that time."

"Which part is the scariest? Is there something that incites fear the most?"

"Close your eyes. Tell me about this moment."

My therapist already knows some of the details—I was asked to join my then best friend and their family on a summer trip, only to find myself in the middle of nowhere. No phone to call for help, no moving without someone watching. It is here my humanity is shredded and discarded on the floor.

But it's the tent that incites the fear. Without enough beds in a crowded house we sleep outside, just the two of us. Before me, the tent ceiling; behind me, the sleeping bag; to my left, a tent wall; to my right, that best friend's arm unzipping my sleeping bag, reaching in and pulling me to them, consuming me. Their words and movements penetrate me and build the monument inside; their smile compels my eyes to look at the choice I had made to lie still and not fight. Our friendship became a contract written on my tongue by theirs. Shame is my shackle, fear is my leash.

It is two weeks of being taken over by night and treated like I do not exist during the day. Invasion became isolation became invasion became isolation. At one point the arms look merciful, comforting me from the sharp feeling of not existing. Two weeks roil like dark waves in my soul, formless and unending, in the arms of a captor I fear to escape.

I become locked on the memory of me apologizing to the arm that pulled me in. *I'm sorry.* It beats against my skull. I didn't know I was tempting you. If only I could give you the answers you wanted, about yourself and your feelings. I am trapped in this cycle of illogical self-destruction.

Her disembodied voice enters the trauma.

"I want you to open your eyes and think about this memory. Follow my fingers and let your mind go where it needs to."

The fear becomes disrupted as my eyes open and follow the fingers. Left, right, left, right, like an eraser. My shoulders drop, the tight feeling in my throat loosens. For the first time since they took hold, those arms around me do not move as I get up.

"Breathe in. Tell me what's going through your mind."

The voice that comes out of me is logical. I tell her I realize I have been given the perspective denied to me by my captivity in the tent.

"Focus on that." The fingers clear the path.

I wander around the memory. Danger is frozen in place like figures at a wax museum. I go to the railroad tracks and the cornfields, all through the house, seeking the right solution, those fingers leading me on. This dark trauma becomes a well-lit memory.

The hour is almost up by the time I return to the tent. The child left in those arms has a conversation with the adult she becomes. She understands she must return to those arms, that she will get through it, that no decision was a good one. Across my mind, all thoughts conclude in unison that she, that I, am freed from the sin of making the wrong choice. She returns to her place in those arms in that tent, but the lights are on, and her agency lays with her. I return to the monument where my therapist waits.

"How are you feeling?"

"We can continue next week if you feel ready for it."

"You did so well."

There are no words to tell her my amazement. The appointment concludes and I go to my car with the taste of saltwater on my tongue.

MIRANDA HUGHES (Salt City Scribes) is a storyteller who combines casual behavior analysis with synesthesia to break into your psyche and leave a tale stained in your grey matter. She also enjoys deconstructing fantasy as a side hobby. When not writing stories she's making interactive fiction through Dungeons & Dragons campaigns and creating story mods for video games. Her short fiction piece "The Color of Sinew" and her poem "Asexual Benediction" were published in the University of Utah's literary journal *The Canticle* in 2017. Follow her antics on Twitter at @mahugheswrites, where her story will grow more interesting as she pursues her MA in English-Writing at Salem State University this Fall 2020.

Lessons on America

Jayrod P. Garrett

Dear Students,
the pilgrims who established
this nation did not steal.
Stealing is against the law;
God's law. And they wouldn't do that.
So instead they codified
trade across the ocean
with people at war with each other;
made agreements
bound in unreadable law
to liberate them from their enemies;
establishing points of contact
on all sides. Offering new lives
to those they captured
across the ocean where
they would be able to live
as God intended. Except when
they were cheated; God and law
justified the seizure

of the black man serving
as their point of contact.

My students,
imagine yourselves
sprinting across the plains of Africa
to protect your tribe from raiders,
hunting and feasting with your family,
and telling your friends stories of a star-filled sky.
And now you are chained by foreigners,
given tainted water, spoiled food,
and living in cramped darkness.
When your captors burn your skin
with water to cleanse you,
they rationalize that God
has forsaken you
as they roll your dead family into the ocean.
They beat you for your mourning.
They whip you out of shape and tell you
in words you cannot understand
to be healthy, hale, and whole.
What few of you arrive
in America everyone knows
in language clearer
than holy writ
you're a field animal.

Sorry students,
genocide is a subject we study
from foreign nations, not our own.
There is no genocide of cattle.
Cattle may have families, but not history.
So you sell their children.
You sell their partners.

But you recognize their intelligence.
You manipulate their emotions
to increase production– this is being a
good steward. You give them
your religion, your language,
your society and culture.
Punish them when you hear them moo.
Cattle don't have that freedom.
Because they cannot understand their strength
that fifty of them is more than eight of you
and they are well armed and muscled
by their work for you.
You milk them like cattle
using them to build
your own promised land.

Students! Students!
You have so many questions!
But we aren't going to answer them.
Our law has no place
to acknowledge the wrongs
of the past. Nor means to
fix the consequences
of our founding father's actions.
That would mean we have
to reconsider what humanity is,
or honor that above
our precious past.
You see, if we consider history
as whole, offer to those
without such a claim
on that truth, we must
acknowledge the benefits
we have from past cruelties.

And if our ancestors taught us
anything, it was this:
To pass the buck,
manipulate the truth,
and keep our hands clean.
This is scripture.
This is Godly.
This is the American Law.

JAYROD P. GARRETT (Salt City Scribes, Salt City Genre
Writers) is a performance poet and storyteller from Ogden,
Utah. As a Black man living in Utah, he's long felt alone in a
culture that demanded his assimilation for survival. This is one
of the reasons he went to Weber State University to get his
degree in English to develop his own voice that he could be his
own person. In an effort to share what he learned there he
spent four years running an open mic in Ogden called Voices.
Inspired by current events he's engaged in a new project
developing Utah's first Black Artist Collective while working on
his first novel. He lives in Bountiful with his wife Melissa and
their two sons. You can find his poetry and blogs at:
jayrodpgarrett.com.

Sleeping Alone: The Wife Left Behind

C.H. Lindsay

Beside me,
the lifeless pillow
    lurks,
an effigy of
    my fallen love.

The framed flag
atop my mantle
    looms,
a constant emblem
    of ultimate service.

The formless blanket
on his empty chair
    skulks:
a constant symbol
    of unattainable warmth.

The ghostly memories
trapped in the cracks of my heart
    mock
my lonely home
    with empty tomorrows.

C.H. LINDSAY (Infinite Monkeys) is primarily a stay-at-home wife and mother. She is also an actress, conrunner, poet and writer. Of late, she spends most of her time being a hermit in her "mom cave" where she writes and runs an online text-based role-playing fleet of sci-fi simulations. She also collects books. Lots and lots of books. She is a member of SFWA, HWA, SFPA, and LUW.

Freedom Listed in the Classifieds

Erica Swenson

"Hold it steady!" Pyper's mom, Sylvia Durand, called with the authority of a sea captain. The flesh behind her arms swung in rhythm with the jack.

Dutifully Pyper braced herself to prevent any tipping. The jack leveled with the step, and the piano rolled forward with a jangle of keys, hammers, and wires. Pyper threw her weight against the top while her mother repositioned the jack and blocks and started the process again. There were six steps up to the second level, and it had taken them half an hour to get to this last one. Pyper's arms ached and little drops of sweat flicked off her mother's forehead to patter like rain on the pavement. The jack lifted as the piano dangerously teetered. With a grunt, Sylvia gave a final push on the handle, and the piano eased onto the level ground. Pyper imagined that even the wooden instrument sighed as it settled onto stable footing.

Pyper took the front and Sylvia pushed from the back as they walked along the sidewalk. She found her door and felt a little thrill when her key worked. This was hers. She had to share it with three other girls, but this little apartment could be whatever she wanted it to be. The piano bumped over the threshold.

Sylvia directed her to an open wall. They used the jack one more time to get the wheels out and the musical beast settled into place.

"Now remember, you are here for one purpose: to perform. We've come so far and you are so close. I want you to spend at least four hours a day practicing. Do what's necessary to pass your other classes, but you have got to glow like an atomic bomb for your piano teachers. Only the best make this happen," Sylvia instructed as she leaned against the top for support.

"Yes, Maestro," Pyper said.

"Good. Let's go get the rest of your stuff."

"Thanks, Mom," Pyper said with a loving smile.

It was a strange distinction they followed. Her mom had insisted that when it came to the piano, she needed to be respected and obeyed. The term "Maestro" gave her authority, so that's what Pyper called her. Maestro insisted she spend hours practicing, even withholding dinner if she refused. Mom was the woman who took her to parks, museums, and concerts. Mom made her manicotti for her birthday, and when she was little, tickled her before she went to sleep. It would have been easier if they were two separate people so she could be infuriated with one and love the other. Instead, they were a packaged deal, and Pyper had learned to differentiate between what each expected of her.

The rest of her stuff came up in just a few trips. With no sign of her new roommates, Pyper claimed her bed and threw her bedspread across it. Black and white piano keys ran from the head to the foot. She artfully hung up her display board with her competition medals and ribbons. Sylvia lined up her trophies on a shelf, tallest in the middle and tapering off, just like they'd stood at home in their living room.

Finished with the bedroom, Pyper followed her mom to the door.

"Your account has enough money for a month. Don't waste any or you'll be hungry by the end. I want a phone call every night. No excuses." Her mom gave her a refined bow with a straight back and ninety degree bend at her waist, and Pyper mimicked the movement with a practiced one of her own.

Sylvia let herself out. Pyper listened as her footsteps receded. Unable to contain herself, she squealed with glee, jumped, and shook her hands. She threw open the industrial curtains and let in the sunshine. The light reflecting from the black glossy surface of the piano almost made it seem friendly. Pyper turned away to investigate her new home. She opened all of the cupboards. They were empty, but full of potential. The fridge had an abundance of potential as well.

Her stomach reminded her that breakfast had been hours and one piano move ago. She could fix that. She grabbed her purse and headed out the door. The grocery store was a block away and slightly downhill. An abandoned shopping cart sat on the sidewalk. Pyper pointed the wheels forward and stepped onto the back. Her chariot coasted down the path. She threw her arms out wide and closed her eyes. Sunshine warmed her chestnut hair and the wind caressed her cheeks. The wheels clicked and clacked over the seams in the sidewalk with an accelerating beat.

The beat stopped with a bang as the cart jerked to a stop and she nearly went headfirst into the basket. She'd hit the parking barrier by the grocery store. She quickly looked around to see if anyone had seen her. The handle may have bruised her ribs, but at least her ego was still intact. She brushed her hair away from her face and swept into the store like the elegant diva she'd been trained to be.

First stop was the produce section. Sylvia insisted Pyper look as lovely as she sounded. In a competition where so much was subjective, first impressions were crucial. Dinners were filled with couscous, quinoa, avocados, and chicken. The refrigerator was always packed with carrot and celery sticks, and there was a precise little plastic cup she could fill once a day with ranch. Dutifully Pyper filled her cart with fresh fruits and veggies. Then her eyes strayed.

The bakery was strategically located next to the produce. Glistening in their case, the donuts called to her. Unable to stop them, her feet left the cart behind and carried her over. Powder, sprinkles, frosting, and glaze beckoned her. Something that sweet, fatty, and unnecessary had been forbidden. Her mother never brought them home, so she had never even tried them. Occasionally she'd sampled a cookie if it had been part of refreshments after a concert, but never a fried donut.

Selfconsciously Pyper looked around. There was no one here to stop her. Timidly she grabbed a sheet of wax paper and picked out a donut. Dark chocolate frosting was flecked with orange and blue sprinkles to celebrate the local college. She was just showing her school spirit, she reasoned with herself. One bite and she'd pay for it and finish her shopping. Her teeth sunk into the soft sweat dough. The frosting melted in her mouth and she discovered a delectable cream in the middle. The next bite happened without conscious thought. She wanted this, she needed this, and she was appalled she had spent her whole life without this.

She rushed to the self-checkout stands. The last thing she needed was for her mother to bail her out of jail for stealing a donut. Paid for, her treat vanished seconds later. Pyper went back to her abandoned shopping cart and the donut case. A handy box held a dozen. She filled it with one of each variety.

The grocery store stretched before her filled with new wonders. She found ice cream and frozen dinners in the freezer aisle. Sweet breads were just a short ways away from the gluten-free whole grain loaves her mother had always insisted on. There were too many chips to choose from. She decided to go by color and try a purple bag first.

Dinner that night was salad and donuts. She ate alone in her apartment, but she wasn't completely alone. The piano brooded in the living room. When her mother was at work, a piano had always been there, her captor and her freedom. She hadn't gone to public school. Maestro had insisted it wouldn't leave her enough time to practice and she would learn more working on her own. The instrument at home was a grand piano that filled the living room. A couch huddled against the wall beside it, an invader in the piano's domain.

This instrument was an upright, like a grand lady with her massive skirts tucked in close. It was a gift from her mother for going to college. Pyper approached the new piano like it was a rabid animal ready to bite. She pulled out the bench and positioned it at the precise distance from the keyboard. A quick glance around confirmed no one was watching.

A sweet teddy bear had always glared at her when she was growing up. Maestro was always watching from her desk at work through the camera in its beady eyes. Pyper would practice hours a day and dreaded the crackle that would erupt from that furry belly. "Fingers curved, back straight. That measure is sloppy, play it again." When Maestro was home there were demonstrations of how to play better, and there was always a better.

Sylvia had dreamed of being a concert pianist, but she had started too late. The kids her age at competitions had started playing at four, and she could never catch up, so she was left behind. She reminded Pyper she would not have to suffer the same fate. Together they had excelled at recitals and contests. Pyper would stand for her bows and would always see her mother standing at the side of the stage enjoying the applause as well. They had applied for Juillard. After the audition, they were gently informed that Pyper's technique was flawless, but there was no emotion in her music. They didn't have a spot for her.

Her mother raged and then applied for Pyper to go to the University. They had a good music program and would be able to give her more individual attention. She'd vowed they would prove those Julliard snobs that the best pianists could come from other schools.

So here Pyper was, staring at her new piano. The bear was gone, and she could do whatever she wanted this evening. She sat on the bench and settled her fingers on the keys. Her shoulders relaxed and she consciously allowed her back to slouch. She skipped the warm-up scales and arpeggios. Instead, she played simple songs she'd memorized years ago. She plucked out the melody and added her own variations to movie theme songs. Then she just let her fingers choose. The notes told a story of her frustrations: the hours alone to study and practice, watching kids from her window laughing together as they walked to school, a childhood devoid of donuts, the mother she loved, and the Maestro that drove her on.

A pounding sounded on the wall. "Hey, we're trying to sleep," someone shouted from next door. Pyper had lost track of time. Embarrassed she stood from the bench and went to bed.

The next day was filled with student orientation and exploring campus. She found all of her classrooms including a lecture hall for Biology that was bigger than many of her concert theaters. The music department had little practice rooms with pianos. That would come in handy if she needed to do any more late-night rehearsing.

Her wallet cried a little when she bought all of her textbooks. Who knew bundles of paper could cost so much? There was something magnificent about them. History was a required class, and the textbook gleamed under her fingers. She opened it up, skimmed through the vivid pictures, and started to read the text. She found stories of battles and wars and the wild leaders that fought them. Brave men and women had stories even more daring than what she'd found in novels.

Part of her musical instruction was learning the history of the composers. She'd learned about Haydn and Bach the way other kids heard stories of Cinderella and Snow White. She loved how it made the names human. Her history book sparked that same sense of wonder and connection. She found herself on the floor next to the fudge counter happily reading with her feet tucked in so she wouldn't trip anyone. When an employee tapped her shoulder and pointed out a bench across the store, Pyper decided it was her cue to leave.

At home, Pyper was surprised to discover her piano had grown a TV. Resting on the top was a large flat screen that hung six inches off of each side. Playing on the TV, a larger than life mom and daughter were arguing about a $20,000 wedding dress.

"I knew someone else was here. The sink was already filled with dishes," a girl said as she entered the room. Her hair was swept up in a turban, and she wore a blue silk robe even though Pyper could see long fleece pajama bottoms underneath. She walked like a model, but there was something about her face that broke the illusion. Pyper couldn't put her finger on it. Maybe her eyes were too close together or her nose was turned up too far. Or maybe it was the scowl her features seemed permanently pulled into. Pyper dubbed her the "bathrobe diva," but knew better than say it out loud.

"Taffeta" the girl announced and held out her hand as if she were a princess waiting for it to be kissed. Pyper awkwardly took it and gave it two firm shakes before letting it go.

"Pyper."

"This must be your instrument. It takes up half the room."

"This must be your TV. I'm glad you were able to find a place for it."

"I'm sure we'll have a lovely year together. I took a bed in the other room. We'll see who else comes home today. By the way, it's courteous to do your own dishes," Taffeta said over her shoulder as she sauntered to the bathroom.

Pyper went to the sink and quickly washed her dishes. The TV continued to blare as the two tried to decide between the modern dress the bride loved and the princess dress that was the mother's dream. If the mother loved the bride, she'd make her happy on her wedding day. The mother pointed out she was paying for this and if the bride loved her and had any sense she would agree. The saleswoman was just trying to convince someone to buy something. In the end the two left the store in a huff without a dress. Everyone was unhappy. A teaser flashed across the screen before commercials that they would be back to look for the perfect dress in the next segment.

Taffeta was still in the bathroom. Pyper could hear the blow dryer. She had to practice, so she went over to the piano and pulled out the bench. She left the TV on, but easily ignored it and started to play. She made it through the first measure of Rachmanioff before the storm hit.

"What are you doing?" Taffeta shrieked as she came around the corner. Half of her blonde hair hung in a wave of curls while the rest was lax and straight.

Pyper looked stunned. "I'm practicing"

"But I'm watching my show," Taffeta exclaimed and gestured at the monstrosity perched on the piano top.

Pyper stood up and pushed in the bench. Satisfied that she'd made her point, the Bathrobe Diva left the room. Unsure what to do with herself since she couldn't practice, Pyper pulled out her history book again.

Attila the Hun was invading Italy when her other two roommates arrived. Claire reminded Pyper of a mouse with her tiny nose turned up and her thin almost grey air hanging limply down around her slender shoulders. Even her squeaky soprano voice added to the resemblance. Bayley would have fit in with the basketball players but she didn't make the cut. Somehow she clipped the light in the living room with her head and banged her knee against the piano bench right after. Pyper got her a bag of ice and helped everyone carry their stuff in while Taffeta finished her hair in the bathroom.

After getting everyone moved in, someone knocked on the door. Pyper knew it wasn't more roommates—the apartment was full. She cracked open the door and glanced out. Boys! The doorway was full of them. What should she do? Was there something she was supposed to say? She opened the door the rest of the way and managed to squeak out a "Hi" that sounded a lot like Claire. Boys were strictly forbidden at home, but now a pack of them stared at her.

"Is Tafetta home?" the front one asked. He must be the leader, Pyper thought, but that was about as far as her thinking could go.

"Hi, Garth. Come in," Tafetta said. Her bold makeup and perfectly primped hair made her look like an actress from a movie. Pyper backed off in relief and a little disappointment. Tafetta introduced the guys from 210.

"We're heading to the Sweetwater. Anybody want to come with us?" Garth asked.

All eight of them managed to pack into Ryan's minivan. Claire fit in the trunk and Bayley got shotgun. Piper was wedged between Grayson and James and couldn't have been happier. She had no idea what to say, but just being in the van with everyone laughing around her was fun.

They pulled up to the Sweetwater and her heart dropped.

"It's a bar." Pyper pointed out.

"More like a pub." Garth corrected.

"I'm too young to drink."

"We're not here for the beer. They serve the best burgers and french fries in town."

They were right. The burgers and fries were amazing. She discovered Bayley could tell stories that would make you laugh so hard you couldn't sit up straight. Claire turned the napkins into birds, buildings, goalposts, and balls for the guys to play with. Tafetta could carry on a conversation even without anyone else there. Once Pyper got her voice working, she could talk to the boys and they could talk to her like anyone else.

That night she lay quietly in bed waiting for sleep with a smile on her face.

Then her phone rang. It was her mom. Oops! She remembered too late that she was supposed to check in.

"Hi, Mom," Pyper answered.

"It's Maestro. What were you thinking! A bar? You spent my money to go drinking in a bar. We haven't been working for years for this to have you ruin everything by partying. It's a Thursday." Her mom continued to rant as Pyper tried to get an explanation in between the yelling. She looked over at the bed next to hers, and Claire gave her a sleepy glance. She took her shrieking phone and headed for the bathroom which would hopefully muffle the conversation.

"There was no alcohol involved, Maestro. We just had dinner there," Pyper finally managed to sneak in.

"How can I possibly believe you? All I see is a charge for $11.63. That's plenty for a few shots of tequila. You meet your teacher in the morning. You should have been practicing instead of going out." Maestro was clearly mad, but her ranting took a turn for the worst.

"I knew this was a bad idea. I'm coming to get you in the morning. You will stay here where I can watch you and ensure that progress is made and no more mistakes happen."

Pyper's stomach dropped like a roller coaster and twisted itself into knots. The last few days had been liberating, and she didn't want to step back into her chains.

"You don't need to do that. I'll behave." Pyper said. Grudgingly Maestro agreed to give her a second chance and hung up.

The next day, her meeting with her teacher went smoothly. She played through her concert pieces flawlessly, and the grey-haired woman quietly applauded her in the small practice room. "Everything was played with perfection, but it all lacked enthusiasm." Ouch.

Hours later she was still in the practice room trying to force enthusiasm into the music she'd played a hundred times.

But Pyper was preoccupied. The credit card in her purse felt like a plastic spy that ratted on her whenever she stepped out of line.

Fortunately salvation came with pizza. A flyer outside the student union offered a free pizza if you signed up for a student bank account. The pizza warmed her tummy, and the little bit of plastic had her name on it. She would banish the spy when she got back to her apartment.

She still had a problem, though. The little card was only worth what she deposited in the account. Right now her childhood piggy bank held more bacon, and that wouldn't pay for a donut run.

Buoyed by her first successful step to self-sufficiency, Pyper decided to do a little exploring to see if she could take another. Many of the campus jobs were already filled. She hopped the free shuttle to downtown. What did she want to do? She'd never asked herself this before. Her days were filled with music and her ambitions had been defined for her. Now her life, or at least her college job, was open. From the streets she walked, Pyper spotted signs looking for waitresses or cashiers. People were out walking handfuls of dogs that looked like they were attempting to wrap their walker like ribbons around a maypole. Maybe she could start her own little business. Professionals in suits and pencil skirts walked purposefully from taxis into tall gleaming buildings. Pyper thought she'd look good in a suit.

As she was considering working at a bakery and getting her donuts for free, destiny almost ran her over. Luckily it honked first so she could get back onto the curb in time.

The old army transport had been repurposed into an urban safari experience. The exterior was painted in a zebra print, but instead of black and white, it was gray and purple. The sides were rolled up to let in the unseasonably warm autumn air. The wonder-filled faces of tourists drank in the sight of the tall buildings while the guide in the front pointed out the sights and kept up a dialogue of history and stories.

"The statue on your right dates back to the founding of the city. I know it seems silly to commemorate a turkey, but if Mr. Sawyer hadn't been out turkey hunting, he wouldn't have found the gold that brought everyone else here."

Pyper could hear the woman from her spot on the sidewalk. She'd absent-mindedly started to cross the road without looking for traffic. Now that she was looking, she spotted a large help wanted sign hanging on the back. The white stood out boldly from the stripes. Grabbing a pen from her bag, she wrote the number on her hand. Her time was ticking. She had to call there on the sidewalk before she washed her hands again.

"I'm calling about the job," Pyper tried to sound confident as she spoke into the phone. She wasn't even sure what type of job they were offering. Mostly she wanted to finish hearing the story of Mr. Sawyer and his turkey.

"Wonderful. We're short on tour guides. I can give you an interview right now," the chipper woman on the phone said.

Wasn't she supposed to do a resume first, or something like that? The lady at the other end of the line couldn't see Pyper's bewilderment.

"We always screen our applicants with one request. Tell me a story." There was an awkward silence as the lady politely waited for a response.

"Uh . . . what?"

"A story. Any old story would do. Your favorite bedtime story, something funny that happened to you, you could even tell me about Jack and Jill, but spice it up a bit. Our tour guides have to be engaging, so that's how we measure the people who apply."

Pyper was at a loss. If this was a piano audition, she had a dozen pieces she could play. Her personal life was rather dull; there was no interesting material there. There was only one topic that she knew really well.

"Once upon a time there was a man named Beethoven. People like to tell about how he was a great composer, yet some of his best music was written after he went deaf. Most people don't know about the tragic history of his heart."

On the spot she took the dry facts she knew about Beethoven's love for an aristocratic woman, the Countess Josephine Brunswick, to create a story. "She started out as his piano student, but their feelings grew beyond the lessons. Although their love might endure, their relationship could not. It was arranged that Josephine would marry another, Count Deym. In the stories, the ill-fated lovers find a way to their happily ever after, but in life, practicality is too strong of a pull. Josephine married and had three children with one more on the way when Count Deym died of illness. Once again the love of Beethoven and Josephine flared. Passionate letters crossed back and forth. But, alas, his commoner status could not be overcome. Pressure from her family tore them apart, and once again she married an aristocrat. In the end, they died apart and alone."

"You're hired."

Back at her apartment, Pyper was greeted by sparkling little girls prancing across the stage in glittering crowns. They were taller on the huge screen then they would have been in real life.

Taffeta was enrobed in pink today and was painting her toenails on the couch.

"Pass me that book over there," Taffeta gestured.

Compliantly Pyper picked up the math book and took it over. She expected Taffeta to read it, but instead she slipped it under her toes to prevent any paint from dripping.

Pyper turned on her computer at the kitchen table. Guilt dragged on her. There was an almost physical pull drawing her to the piano, but then she would have to face the wrath of Taffeta. She dismissed the urge and engrossed herself in the information from her new job the secretary had emailed. She read stories of the founding of the city. She'd never known there had been a flood years ago and they had turned Main Street into a river to drain the town. There was a hole in the bricks of one of the older buildings. Someone had mistaken a live round for a dud during a military parade, and as a reminder to the world to double-check your work, they'd left the hole.

When Pyper arrived at work the next day, she expected to shadow for a few days, but they threw her on a bus of her own. Initially terrified, Pyper reminded herself that she'd performed for much larger and more critical audiences. She happily retold all of the stories she'd learned the night before.

She was a natural, but it took a lot of work. She had torn through all of the study material they sent her and practiced her delivery at the mirror in the girl's bathrooms on the top floor of the engineering building. She rarely saw anyone else there. Tourists gave her glowing reviews, and her tours filled to overflowing.

Between classes and work, she had less time to practice. It didn't help that much of her practice time was early or late when she didn't want to disturb her neighbors or Taffeta, who had claimed the armchair in the living room in her robes of many colors and would squawk whenever Pyper started to play.

Her first paycheck arrived. If she was careful, it was just enough money to cover her living expenses. She wouldn't have to use Maestro's money. The pressure constraining her every day of her life eased. She could do this on her own.

There was a note with the check. "We're hosting a tour of Europe. Since you are not a senior guide, we can't fully pay for your trip. If you can provide airfare and help with luggage and logistics, we can pay for everything else. The world is yours."

Never in Pyper's life had she wanted anything more. The energy of her competitions and performances was nothing compared to the thrill she had on her tours. This European tour would be the highlight of her life so far.

She didn't have the money. Plane tickets weren't cheap. She was already working all of the hours she could get and was barely passing her classes. Her piano teacher not only complained about her lack of enthusiasm but commented on the quality of her performances as well.

She looked at the black beast against the wall. Instead of its shiny new keys, she'd spent more time playing the grubby ones at the practice lab. She was using it as an over-priced TV stand. Her stomach twisted like the spinach linguine she'd eaten through childhood. Could she do it?

A quick picture with her phone and a short paragraph on the right webpage, and her life was forever altered.

Pyper didn't feel very different when she went to the counselor's office and changed her major from music to history. The trip to Europe was eye-opening, but not life-altering. It wasn't even when she and her mother buried Maestro. It was a rather loud funeral with lots of yelling, but the pent up feelings were finally loose to dissipate in the wind. Freedom came the day movers took the piano away, that last reminder of her stolen childhood and misplaced dreams. Her constant friend and oppressor jangled down each step. The notes of the many songs she'd played flowed through her head, but now they filled her with enthusiasm.

ERICA SWENSON (The Herriman Chapter) is a new writer. A mom of three busy boys, she still tries to find time for reading, running, and playing her bagpipes.

An Infatuation with Light

Shirley Manning

Everything is illuminated –
in a lightning strike
that reveals the door
leading out of the little room
where I keep myself –
with an imagined dead bolt
that locks me in from
joyful liberation?
exquisite danger?

And then –
the inevitable boom of thunder
insisting I open my eyes –
break the lock
open the door
walk through –
and become the key on a kite,
soaring into the tempest
of a chaotic sky.

From author **SHIRLEY MANNING**:
I am delighted to be included in this anthology, celebrating eighty-five years of The League of Utah Writers. The League, its members and opportunities to learn about writing in a variety of ways—chapter meetings, conversations, conferences and critical feedback on my own writing—have been a great support to me in my romance with words. I'd also like to take this opportunity to thank my fellow writers for their beautiful contributions to this special anthology and to thank those who have extended their talents and efforts to create and publish *The Function of Freedom.*

Rights

Valarie Schenk

People everywhere
deserve unequivocal
access to be free.

VALARIE SCHENK (Blue Quill) is a creative based in Roy, Utah who serves through art and writing in order to assign meaning to personal experiences and communicate lessons learned through living. It is her deepest desire that these efforts promote and create safe spaces where people can connect with one another and heal alongside a friend. Learn more about Valarie on Instagram at @valarieschenk5898 or search her name on Facebook.

UTAH WRITERS' ROUNDUP SET AUGUST 10, 11

E. S. Gardner Scheduled On Program, Chairmen Of Groups Named

Plans for the Utah Writers' Roundup at the Ben Lomond hotel August 10 and 11 under the sponsorship of the Blue Quill chapter, Ogden unit of the League of Utah Writers' are under way, it was announced Saturday by Mrs. Larry P. Wright, president of the Ogden unit and general chairman of arrangements.

Morning and afternoon meetings will be held on both days, with luncheon meetings during the noon hours being planned, Mrs. Wright said. Other entertainment features are to be worked out by the various committees.

Program Arranged

The full program will be mapped out under the chairmanship of Frank Robertson of Springville, president of the state organization, and Mrs. Roland Knowles of Ogden, while Mrs. Florence S. Glines is chairman of the refreshments and decorations committee.

Lewis J. Wallace, Ogden city attorney, will be toastmaster at the first noon luncheon meeting.

Earl Stanley Gardner, popular "slick" magazine writer who contributes to Colliers, Saturday Evening Post, Liberty and other national magazines, announces he will make every effort to attend at the convention. He is among the "big names" scheduled to make a talk.

Committee Chairmen

Chairmen of other committees include: Mrs. Wilson K. Anderson, reservations; Mrs. M. S. Stone, advertising and printing; Mrs. Dave Wangsgaard, poets' breakfast on August 11; and Mrs. K. A. Bleeker, luncheon arrangements, all of Ogden.

Free copies of Author and Journalist magazines will be given to those who attend.

The Ogden Standard-Examiner | July 15, 1940

The Thing Inside Jacky Jensen's Garage

Caryn Larrinaga

Missy's bolt cutters pinched at the padlock on the garage's side door. When she pulled them away, a thin groove betrayed our unsuccessful efforts to cut the lock free.

There was no walking away now. Even if we couldn't get in, Jacky Jensen would know somebody had tried to access his garage.

If he figured out who it was, we were dead. He'd dislocated my shoulder in this same driveway fifteen years ago, and that'd just been for "trespassing" on his property while trying to retrieve Missy's favorite Frisbee.

I rubbed my shoulder and cast a nervous glance at the dark street behind us. "Hurry up. They'll notice we're gone any minute."

Missy grunted and squeezed the bolt cutters again, bracing one handle against her chest and using both arms to pull the other toward her body. Her blonde curls fell into her face as she strained the muscles that had helped earn her a scholarship to Southern Utah University. "It might . . . help . . . ," she panted, "if you . . . push . . . too."

I silently disagreed. My palms were way too sweaty to grip anything. Besides, this had been her idea.

Well, not the part about the breaking into Jacky's garage. That'd been mine. But I'd wanted to go to Home Depot, get some industrial-strength bolt cutters, and then just take them back for a refund after. Missy vetoed me, insisting we use her dad's rusty old pair so there wouldn't be any retail security footage that could tie us to the crime.

Crime. The word sent a jolt of fear into my belly. What if Jacky bailed on the party and came home early? What if he called the cops?

"Screw this," I said. "Let's get out of here."

Missy shook her head and spoke through gritted teeth, still winded from the exertion of squeezing the bolt cutters. "Not without . . . a picture . . . of that thing."

The wind picked up as she worked, sending frigid December air down the back of my hooded jacket. I tugged my beanie down over my ears and wondered if the low temperature was making the metal stronger. Before I could chip my way through the layer of Smirnoff Ice that covered the memories of my freshman physics class, a snap and a clink signaled Missy's success.

She groaned and rubbed her sternum through her puffy winter coat. "Ugh, that hurt."

I stared at the break in the padlock's U-bolt, unsure if it would still be "breaking and entering" if we didn't actually *enter* the garage. Missy had no such reservations, quickly yanking the lock away and turning the handle.

"Wait." I pressed a hand against the door. "What if there's nothing in there?"

"Don't puss out on me, Leah."

"I'm not scared! I'm just being pragmatic. Jacky's a liar, and we both know it. Remember when he told us his drum kit cost a hundred grand? And then gave Bruce Higgins a concussion when he called bullshit?"

"This is different." Missy's cheeks burned, either from the cold or the alcohol or both. "If it wasn't true, Jacky would've been bragging about it to everybody. But I only overheard him whispering about it to Michael Birmingham in the bathroom because they didn't know I was behind the shower curtain."

I raised an eyebrow. "Don't tell me you still take shots in the bathtub at parties."

"Don't judge me! You know I don't like the face whiskey makes me make. The point is, Michael's dad works for Weber County Animal Control, so he has access to those trucks with all the cages, right? Jacky probably wants Michael to borrow one so they can move the monster." She scrunched up her face, frowning deeply. "Although . . . it is aquatic. I wonder if they'll stick a kiddie pool in the back of the truck or something to keep it wet."

I rolled my eyes. "Don't be dumb. It's not the Bear Lake Monster. That thing's an urban legend, and a lazy one at that. Like the thing in Loch Ness would have a cousin in Utah."

"Dude, it is so real! And I'm going to get a picture and sell it to TMZ." She pulled her phone out of her pocket and waved it in front of my face. "Who'll be dumb then, huh?"

"Okay, you're officially too drunk for this. TMZ only cares about Hollywood. And besides, on the way over here you said this is the monkey-lizard those people saw up at the Huntsville cemetery."

"Well, Jacky did say something about hair all over the trunk of his car, so it could be the Huntsville Horror. But he's always been obsessed with the Bear Lake Monster, so it could be that." She shrugged. "One or the other, but probably not both."

I shook my head in mock sadness. "I cannot believe you seriously think there's either a prehistoric lake monster or some kind of mutant on the other side of this door. They're made up, Missy. Just stupid stories to scare stupid kids."

"Don't call me stupid." Her eyes flashed angrily. "And if you're so sure nothing's in there, why did you even come?"

I squeezed my shoulder, letting the tiny spike of pain from the old injury dispel the last traces of my earlier buzz. I suddenly remembered exactly why I'd been so eager to trade the warmth of Daniel Bayard's college-break Christmas party for committing a felony in the freezing cold. "Because Jacky Jensen is a sadistic monster, so on the off chance he really has something—or more likely some*one*—locked in that garage, I came to set them free."

Before the fear of being arrested could take hold, I yanked the bolt cutters out of her hand, sucked in a deep breath of icy air, and pulled open the door.

The dueling scents of lawn clippings and engine oil tickled my nose as I tiptoed into the darkness. Missy's footsteps sounded after me, followed by the soft swish of the door closing behind her. A heartbeat later, her cell phone flashlight swept across the cavernous space.

Like most people in our suburban Ogden neighborhood, Jacky's family clearly thought having a garage was less about protecting their cars and more about storing all the crap that couldn't fit into their house. Missy's light passed over two chest freezers, an enormous tool bench, a towering stack of plastic totes, and a bank-vault-style gun safe before settling on a large cube-shaped object covered with a blue tarpaulin.

Missy elbowed me and whispered, "What is that?"

"I don't know," I whispered back. "Could be anything."

"Go look under the tarp."

"*You* go look under the tarp."

Missy's retort died on her lips as a dry, rasping moan drifted across the garage from the cube in the corner. Something metal rattled, and the tarp shifted slightly.

Every hair on the back of my neck pressed upward against my beanie as a shiver that had nothing to do with the temperature shook my body. My hand closed around the door handle behind us.

"Help me . . . " a high voice wheezed. "Please."

"Oh my God," I muttered, releasing the handle and sprinting across the concrete floor. I'd known Jacky was a monster, but this was beyond anything I had ever imagined him capable of doing. Kidnapping a kid and stashing him under a tarp in his garage? That was pure evil.

Missy's light followed me, but she stayed within arm's reach of the door, half crouched like she was ready to leap outside at the next sign of danger. That same metallic rattle sounded again as my fingers closed around the edge of the tarp, and the sharp odor of bleach stung my eyes.

With a single yank, I pulled the tarp to the floor, revealing an enormous dog run with plywood lashed to the top to form a makeshift cage. The flap of the falling fabric wafted the foul stench of urine and feces directly into my face. No amount of bleach could cover that smell, not when the source was exposed to open air. There was another underlying odor there too, something familiar. I gagged, remembering the way my fourth-grade classroom had smelled when we'd gotten lazy about cleaning the class turtle's cage.

As I tugged my scarf up over my nose, Jacky's prisoner darted out of the light with a shriek and huddled against the far corner. If he hadn't just begged for help, I would have assumed he was a large dog from the way he crouched on the ground.

"It's okay!" I told him. "We're not here to hurt you!" Then, without taking my eyes off his unhealthy shape, I called to Missy, "There's another lock here. Keep the light steady."

Either she didn't hear me or she wasn't capable of doing as I asked, because the light shook and shuddered, creating a muted strobing effect. The flashing made it a struggle to fit the blades of the bolt cutter over the small combination lock holding the cage's door closed.

The boy in the corner watched me as I worked. He hid his face behind oversized hands, trembling even harder than Missy. But he seemed to believe what I'd said, inching closer to me as I squeezed the bolt cutters. His outline was strangely fuzzy in the dim light, as though he was covered in a thick layer of cotton.

Or fur.

Bang! Bang! Bang!

The closed metal vehicle door at the front of the garage rattled.

"Hey, you little brats!" a deep voice roared from outside as someone pounded on the door a few more times. "I told you to stay off my property!"

Sweat erupted on my palms. I lost my grip on the bolt cutters and they tumbled out of my hands, clattering to the ground at my feet. I whipped around as the overhead light switched on and the garage door's motor rumbled to life.

The door lifted open, revealing my childhood tormenter an inch at a time: pointed cowboy boots, too-slim jeans, a brown Carhartt jacket, and a thin face too twisted by cruelty to be handsome. Jacky Jensen stood with his hands on his hips, baring his teeth in a snarl.

"Well, well, well. I wondered where you two—" His voice cut off when his eyes landed on the uncovered cage behind me. Rage contorted his features, and a scream ripped from his throat as he lurched toward me. "You stupid bitch! Get away from it!"

I shrieked and ducked, instinctively covering my head with my arms as though this were some kind of impromptu earthquake drill.

Before Jacky finished crossing the garage, something snapped behind me. Metal clinked against metal.

Jacky's sprint slowed. I heard his footsteps falter and dared to look up at him as he skidded to a halt a few feet away from me. The blood drained from his face. His mouth fell open, and a low, frightened moan escaped his lips.

His horrified expression entranced me. I'd never expected to see him look the way he'd made me feel for my entire childhood. Hell, my entire *life.* He'd terrified me until the day I left for college, and only my years out of state had given me enough courage to step foot on his property again.

The cage's door creaked behind me, and the edge of it was suddenly visible at the corner of my vision. Then the beautiful image of Jacky's shocked face was obscured by the lean, dark shape that leaped over me and tackled Jacky to the floor.

Jacky's screams cut through the still night air. I watched, hypnotized, as the fur-covered boy clawed at his captor's face and hands. Blood spattered on the concrete floor. The stink of excrement intensified for an instant, and then I forgot to breathe.

All I could do was watch.

Missy's arms were around me then, hauling me to my feet and yanking me away from the cage. She shouted something I couldn't hear—couldn't process—and I let her pull me back to the side door we'd come through.

As my feet crossed the threshold, Jacky's wails of pain died down to a wet gurgle, then stopped completely.

I paused for one last look at the carnage in his garage. Now that he'd stopped moving, it was easier to make out the shape of the thing Jacky had locked in that cage. His proportions were all wrong; his arms were far too long and his legs far too short to be human. His entire torso was covered in thick, black fur, but when he turned to face me, his features were strangely reptilian, sharp and knobby like a Gila monster.

The thing blinked at me, eyelids closing the wrong way over his slitted pupils. Then, with a final glance back in my direction, the Huntsville Horror shambled off into the night with Jacky Jensen's limp body in tow.

CARYN LARRINAGA (Salt City Genre Writers, Infinite Monkeys) is an award-winning mystery, horror, and urban fantasy writer. Her debut supernatural mystery novel, *Donn's Hill*, was awarded the League of Utah Writers 2017 Silver Quill in the adult novel category and was a 2017 Dragon Award finalist.

Watching scary movies through split fingers terrified Caryn as a child and those nightmares inspire her to write now. Her 90-year-old house has a colorful history, and the creaking walls and narrow hallways send her running (never walking) up the stairs. Exploring her fears through writing makes Caryn feel a little less foolish for wanting a buddy to accompany her into the tool shed.

Caryn lives near Salt Lake City, Utah, with her husband and their clowder of cats. Visit www.carynlarrinaga.com for free short fiction and true tales of haunted places.

Man in the Monster

Tim Heare

Jacob took a deep breath and jerked the heavy door open. He resisted the urge to sneeze as his nostrils filled with dust and the damp smell of wet stone. His prisoner laid facing the wall on the cot his superiors insisted he use.

"Hola," a muffled voice said. "¿Es hora de envenenarme o golpearme?"

"The world would be lucky, but no, there will be no poison or beating today." Jacob just wanted to put a bullet in the man's head and be done with it.

"Ah. Entiendes español mi amigo." The man turned and sat up to get a better look at his jailer.

"Si. Mi español esta bien." Jacob drew out the vowels as they came out of his mouth in a mocking tone.

"My English is good too. Perhaps you would prefer we talk in your language?" The man spread his hands in a wide gesture.

Jacob wanted so badly to grab the man and spit on his face. It would be so easy to take a few steps, let his fingers wrap around the man's neck and shove him into the wall before banging his head against the cement a few times for good measure. But, Jacob had an obligation to the United States, and part of that was ensuring this monster made it to his trial.

When Jacob didn't speak the man leaned back and placed his hands behind his head. "I assume that is dinner?"

"It's more than you served your own guests in this room." Jacob stepped into the ten-foot cell and moved quickly to a small table that had been mounted to the wall. Tonight's dinner included a small piece of chicken, broccoli, salad, and a hunk of bread with butter. He hated that they fed him so well. He didn't deserve it, but they had to keep his strength and stature up for appearances. They needed to show the world they were better than him.

The man leaned forward. "You know who I am, but can I ask your name?"

"I hardly think it matters, senõr." Jacob said.

"If you and I are going to spend time together, it would be easier to use names." The man said.

Jacob pointed to his chest and suppressed a curse. "Lieutenant Smith. But if you expect me to call you President Lopez, you can forget it."

President Lopez stood and gave a slight bow. "I don't think I can claim that title anymore Lieutenant Smith, you may call me Luis."

Jacob turned his back on President Lopez and walked out of the room. He barely registered the two armed guards that stood at attention. Their fingers eased off their triggers as he passed the makeshift guard desk on his way upstairs.

The rough stone stairs opened behind a giant cask in a wine cellar filled with expensive vintages and enough booze to get an entire platoon in trouble. A week ago, servants would keep a steady stream of alcohol flowing to the elite above, while the prisoners below, in Lopez's secret dungeon, would starve and fight off insanity.

He made his way from the wine cellar to the kitchen, and

continued room by room until he reached the grand staircase. The opulence of the palace only fueled his fire as he climbed the curving stairs. Gold gilded the walls and adorned large paintings from throughout history. A crystal chandelier, larger than most cars, hung directly above the staircase, bathing the room in celestial light. The display of wealth made him sick, knowing mere blocks away people starved.

Jacob walked into his assigned bedroom and slammed the door. An ornate painting hit the floor with a bullwhip-like crack. He bent over and picked up the small masterwork, tracing his thumb along the corner where the frame had separated.

With a frustrated scream, Jacob grabbed both sides of the picture and deepened the crack as he pulled the pieces apart. He threw the frame against the wall and watched in shock as the impact shattered what remained, tearing canvas from frame.

He stared transfixed at the ruined painting as his fingers began working through muscle memory to unbutton his stifling fatigues. It was a beautiful work, likely from the seventeen hundreds. A family stood near a pond in their "Sunday best." The little girl's face was filled with joy as her father lifted her high in the air.

Not bothering to remove his opened shirt, he flopped onto the bed and let his gaze follow the blades of the ceiling fan. The circulating air did little to cool the room or his spirit. When his unit came to Uruguay in February the last thing he thought of was summer. Yet here it was, hot as hell with humidity that kept you from ever feeling dry.

The painting reminded him of his family back in Utah. His daughter was the same age as the girl in the painting. It had been over a year since he had seen her. "I'm going to take you on a picnic just like that one when I get home," he said as the fan slowly circled above his head.

Jacob pulled out a photo of his wife and daughter from his breast pocket and gave them a little kiss, closed his eyes, and let himself drift away for a few hours, dreaming of their picnic.

———

It had been a week since their first meeting. Jacob kept his distance, only seeing Lopez when dropping off food, or peeking in his cell periodically to make sure all was as it should be. He liked to think of himself as level-headed, but all he could see when he looked at Lopez were the starved faces he passed from the outskirts of the city to the palace itself. He flipped through his notes as he headed to the cell for another meal.

President Lopez came to rule Uruguay twenty-five years ago when he overthrew a corrupt regime. The people looked forward to his promised democracy, but after his third election it was clear they had merely changed oppressors. Political rivals were jailed, or simply vanished. The economy crashed, while his supporters fattened their wallets and leeched off his power. Lopez blamed foreigners for the increase in crime and short-ages in basic necessities, and after years of oppression, he crossed the line and used chemical weapons to cleanse his country of their filth.

When the coalition finally took the palace and waved their flag, it was clear that their victory didn't compare to Uruguay's loss. The people were promised a quick trial. Jacob's assign-ment was to ensure Lopez's safety until that day, whether it came in six years or six months.

"How are you today?" Lopez asked, as he did with every meal.

Jacob set the tray on the small table and turned to leave.

"¿Tal vex preferirias espanol hoy?" Lopez asked with a slight smile.

"Not in Spanish, not in English." Jacob said walking to the door.

"It's a simple question my friend." Lopez shrugged his shoulders.

"We aren't friends, Mr. Lopez. I have a job to do. Nothing more." Jacob said.

Lopez cocked his head as if considering something. "You're the only face I see anymore. That is the closest thing I have to a friend here. I heard the guards call you Jacob. So, Jacob, please call me Luis."

"I have real friends outside this cell. Less of them thanks to you. But more than you have on this entire planet." Jacob said with a lift of his chin.

Lopez's eyes softened and his mouth opened slightly. "I'm sorry for your loss, Jacob. It is a hard thing to lose someone. I see now why you hate me."

"Don't talk to me about death. You are death itself and I won't take pity from someone who has no soul." Jacob let his words hang in the air then walked out.

Lopez sat quietly on his cot for several days. He kept his head bowed and avoided eye contact with each encounter. Only after Jacob left would he cross the room to get his meal and eat it in silence.

"Jacob, I know I can't ease your pain. But I would like to try." Lopez said during one such breakfast, dispelling an oppressive reticence that had grown to fill the cell.

"Excuse me?" Jacob was surprised to hear him speak after so many days of silence and found himself responding before he could force his mouth shut.

When Jacob didn't say more, Lopez continued. "I understand you may think me a monster. But I am not this thing you think I am. As I see it, we are going to spend a lot of time together, and it doesn't need to be unpleasant for us both."

"No, just unpleasant for you." Jacob paused and considered his next words. "Mr. Lopez."

"Please. Luis." Lopez said.

"Luis." Jacob sighed as the man's name escaped his lips. It opened a pit in his stomach that quickly filled with venom. "You have committed crimes against humanity and are to stand trial. My job here is to see you safely delivered. It's not to entertain you like a guest in my home. I will feed you. I will ensure your safety. Nothing more."

"Well then, I will just have to make do with what little I can get." Lopez moved over to his meal and began to delicately eat like a picky three-year-old.

Several more days passed with the same routine. Lopez would try to start a conversation. Jacob would ignore him. Lopez would quietly eat his food.

"Do you like baseball Jacob? I always liked American baseball." Lopez said one evening as Jacob placed his latest meal on the table.

"I'm not one for baseball. We don't have a team where I'm from." Jacob caught himself from adding more. He found it harder each day to ignore Lopez's prattling.

"I thought all American's had a favorite team. It is America's pastime is it not?" Lopez used his fork to stab a piece of chicken. "I always liked the Los Angeles Dodgers myself. As a child my father would sit with me and watch games on our television. Of course the games had been played weeks before, but that didn't matter."

Jacob remembered watching baseball with his own father.

He always found it boring, but his dad insisted it was the TV that made it boring; live games were much more exciting.

"I always dreamed of seeing Dodger Stadium. I imagined one day I would come to America to meet your President and we would meet in Los Angeles. I would tell him of my love for the Dodgers, and he would arrange for us to sit behind home plate." Lopez looked up toward the ceiling and sighed. "I would bring my granddaughter and buy her, what are they called? Ah yes. Cracker Jack."

"I don't think the President would have welcomed your company." Jacob said.

"Maybe not today, not this new President of yours. But when I was fighting for my country's freedom, your President seemed very welcoming." Lopez popped the chicken into his mouth.

Jacob let out a small laugh. Lopez however just continued to chew as if he didn't get the joke.

"You're serious?" Jacob said.

"Of course. Do you think a poor farmer could build a revolution, let alone arm them? No, my friend. You have your President to thank for that. He helped us stand up. I only spoke with him once, following my election after we won, but his people talked to me more than my madre." Lopez stuck a piece of broccoli into his mouth. "He told me your country owed me a debt, but when I came to collect, his replacement ignored my calls."

"You're saying we owed you a favor, and you called in your chit for a Dodgers Game. You are delusional." Jacob laughed and started to walk out of the cell.

"I called to save my people. The war left us poor and starving. I asked him to feed us. To provide jobs and income to our people. Unfortunately, your country's promises are only good for four years at best." Lopez put his fork down on an empty plate. "Thank you for talking with me today Jacob, it was a pleasure."

That night Jacob couldn't sleep. No matter how hard he tried to push them away, Lopez's words came back with equal force. Using the military's VPN, he began his search hours before dawn. The answers weren't in a search engine, nor on Wikipedia. He found them where truths are buried; conspiracy blogs and darkest corners of the internet.

Specifics varied from one government obsessed whack job to the next, but the facts were clear. Thirty years ago, Uruguay was ruled with an iron fist. Elections were a sham, and people were starving. But what got the USA's attention was recently discovered rare-earth metals.

Twelve of the seventeen rare-earth metals were found in large quantities. In particular Promethium, Neodymium, Yttrium, Terbium, and Uranium were found in larger deposits than China's.

When Uruguay threatened to withhold them from the West and began trade negotiations with Iran and North Korea, the United States did everything in its power to force a change in leadership. They did it through Lopez and left him to piece his country back together. The United States considered it a win-win. Until Lopez decided the deal wasn't benefiting his country and demanded a higher price.

Jacob thought back to when he first heard of Lopez. It was hot and he was sitting in front of a fan, holding his newborn daughter, Julia, trying to keep cool while watching TV. He was too lazy to change the channel when the news came on. A reporter spoke about how the President was placing sanctions on Uruguay due to President Lopez's recent open negotiations with terrorist states. He was appalled that any enlightened country would deal with terrorists, especially after the war, and he hoped President Lopez got what he deserved.

Jacob lingered a little longer before walking in with Lopez's breakfast. He didn't know what he wanted to say, but he knew he had to say something.

"How are you doing today Jacob?" Lopez said.

Jacob thought for another moment then continued into the room, placing the tray on the table. He turned back and looked at Lopez. "How do you sleep at night Lopez?"

"Please, it is Luis." Lopez leaned his back against the wall and turned his head to look at Jacob. "That's kind of you to ask. This cot is not as soft as my bed, but it is better than the dirt I slept on in my youth."

Jacob shook his head. "How do you sleep knowing the things you've done."

"Ah, I was wondering when we would get to this. May I eat while we talk?" Lopez sat up and waited for Jacob's consent before moving to the table. "You want to know how a monster acts like a man."

Lopez picked up a piece of buttered toast and gazed at its crusted surface. "The truth is; the monster doesn't think he is a monster." He took a bite and chewed thoughtfully. "I am a man, just like you Jacob. I find beauty in simple things. I make choices that I think are best. Sometimes they are wrong, but that is what it means to be human, eh?" he paused as if remembering something unwanted. "And of course, I have made hard choices I regret."

Jacob let the fist he had been holding behind his back unclench. "Was starving your own people a 'hard choice'?"

"You don't like baseball, but there's another American

game I enjoy. Do you play checkers Jacob?" Lopez changed the subject while scraping the last of his eggs into his mouth.

"Of course, you enjoy it. You get to be kinged." Jacob said.

"Ah, Jacob does have a sense of humor. I like checkers because you can't win without losing. The secret is sacrificing at the right time." Lopez said.

Maybe a line was being crossed, but he wanted so badly to show Lopez that he was superior. Jacob found that nearly every room in the palace had a checkers set. A detail he had somehow missed during all their time in the place. He chose a traditional one with red and black pieces made of clay and brought it with dinner that night.

"Ah! You found the set given to me by my daughter. It is a good set, no?" Lopez flattened the sheets on his cot and motioned for Jacob to set up the board. "Checkers is a game between friends, so please call me by my name."

Jacob placed his red pieces on the squares and looked up. "Fine Luis, but I get to go first." Jacob lost his first game, and not by a little bit. For each piece he captured, Lopez captured two.

From that evening forward, Jacob brought the checkers set at dinnertime. At first their games were played in silence, often lasting mere minutes. But as the weeks moved on Jacob found their games taking more time as he worked to best Lopez. Luis won most of their games, but Jacob won just enough to keep from feeling the outcome was inevitable.

Lopez seemed to be enjoying himself too. He took every opportunity for conversation during their games. They mainly talked about life's mundane moments. Jacob found that in many ways they shared the same tastes, and often, the conversation would continue after their daily game ended.

Jacob waited outside Lopez's door with lunch when a young private walked up to him with a folded sheet of paper. "This just arrived sir."

Careful not to spill Luis's coffee, Jacob set the tray on the floor and unfolded the letter. 'Lieutenant Smith, As you are aware, our government has been working with the people of Uruguay to establish a free government that can only be brought about through the solid foundation of democracy. The people of Uruguay are preparing for open elections, and would like the shadow of Luis Lopez to be resolved before their new elected leaders take office. As a valued ally in their efforts, we have agreed to move up his trial. Please ensure his well-being is maintained until the day of his reckoning, one week from today. Sincerely…"

Jacob saluted the private, dismissing him, quietly folded the letter, and placed it into his pocket before grabbing the tray. He decided to wait until dinner to tell Lopez the news. He hoped a game of checkers would lessen the blow.

Jacob took a walk in the palace gardens after lunch, hoping it would give him time to think. Just four months ago he would have been happy to deliver the macabre news, and yet, he now feared he wouldn't be able to look Lopez in the eyes.

Jacob was so deep in thought he barely registered a voice calling his name. He looked up in time to keep from colliding with the same private from lunch. The man barely caught his breath enough to salute. "Sir, I've been trying to find you for the last thirty minutes. I need you to come with me."

"Easy soldier, take a breath." Jacob said. His own voice

began to quaver, as the man's frantic demeanor seeped into him.

"You need to come with me sir, back inside. There is an urgent matter that requires your attention." The private couldn't look Jacob in the eyes.

"What is it? Is it Luis?" Jacob was afraid something like this would happen. It was only a matter of time before someone would make an attempt on his life.

"No sir, it's," the private didn't want to be the harbinger of this news. "It's your daughter sir."

Jacob walked into Lopez's cell with dinner and the most extravagant checkers set he could find: a board with inlaid pearl, sapphire, and ruby, with pieces made of gold and silver. Lopez's eyes lit up when he saw it.

"Ah Jacob. You have no idea how much joy you've brought me by bringing this board. My wife gave it to me after my first term in office as a reminder of where we came from, and where we were going. It is all I have left of her." Lopez's eyes began to fill with tears as he brushed his fingers across the board. "Why do I deserve such a gift this evening?"

Jacob placed the dinner tray on the table and moved to the center of the room, unsure of what he should say or do next.

"Well, are we going to play my friend? You can go first of course." Lopez grinned as he set the pieces up, then stopped when he noticed Jacob's statuesque state. "Is something wrong Jacob?"

"It happened so fast." Jacob said.

"What did?" Lopez asked.

"Oh Luis, she's gone." Jacob began to sob. He promised himself he wouldn't let Lopez see him cry, but no force of will could hold back his grief.

"Who Jacob? I'm very confused right now." Lopez stood up and took a step toward Jacob.

"She was in our yard, with her friends, and a car, a man, he jumped the curb and, and he," Jacob couldn't say more.

"Oh no. No. No." Lopez placed his arms around Jacob and tried to comfort his friend. "Did they catch him? He must pay for her life with his own."

Jacob broke free of Lopez's arms and pushed him away. "Pay for her life? I just want my daughter back!"

"And you can't have her because they took her from you. They killed your precious girl and now they need to know that you will stop at nothing until they are wiped from the earth." The room somehow felt darker as Lopez spoke, like the sun setting for a northern winter.

"Luis, it was an accident." Jacob suddenly felt disoriented.

"I freed this country from a mad man. I worked tirelessly to root his corruption from our land. And you know what I found? Corruption can't be removed. So, I did what I needed to do and embraced it to keep our home from crumbling into oblivion. And my people's thanks? They accidently took the ones I loved most in this world and filled their bodies with the same bullets I used to free them." Lopez straightened his posture and puffed out his chest.

"How dare you compare my daughter's death to your lust for power? You talk of freedom, but know nothing of it." Jacob heard the door behind him click open as the guards stepped in to check on the noise.

"I know what freedom truly is, Jacob. Do you?" Lopez sneered.

"Tony Morrison once said, 'The function of freedom is to free someone else.' Something you clearly don't understand." Jacob said.

"You are wrong my friend. The function of freedom is to give hope. To blind us from the reality that we will always be oppressed. Freedom is an illusion." Lopez let the last word drip from his mouth.

Jacob's fist closed Lopez's lips as they uttered the last syllable.

He barely acknowledged the pressure of four hands hauling him off Lopez as he landed blow after blow. Like a curtain being drawn, he became aware of himself standing near the door. One guard pushed him through the threshold while another knelt beside the broken old man on the floor.

"I suppose now is as good a time as any to let you know your trial has been moved up. You'll finally face your people and justice. Enjoy the next seven days." He spat on the ground and stepped out the door.

———

Jacob laid on his bed looking up at the ceiling fan. The blades provided a soft breeze that did nothing to quench the hellfire inside his soul. He watched the shadows in the room grow longer until they bathed the room in darkness. Only then did he reach across the bed and pick up the one thing he had been dreading to hold.

The phone rang four times before it clicked, and he heard his wife's voice come to life. "Jake?" she asked.

"Hey. Are doing you OK?" Jacob said.

"Not really. I'm sitting in her room, smelling her pillow, and hoping she'll be watching cartoons when I wake up." Joan said. "Please tell me you're on your way home."

"I can't," Jacob started to say.

"No Jake. I need you here. Now. You can tell Uncle Sam that I will personally start World War III if you aren't home tomorrow." Joan said.

"It's not that simple." Jacob paused when he heard his wife

sobbing. "We can have her funeral when I get back. It'll only be a week. I promise."

"Just come home, okay?" Joan mumbled

The line clicked, and she was gone. He held the reticent phone to his ear for another ten minutes, before hanging up and letting the ceiling fan lull him to sleep.

Jacob stood outside Lopez's cell. All he needed to do was walk in and leave the food, but even that seemed too much. Instead he handed the tray to a guard, who gave him a surprised look, but understood the situation.

When the door opened and Lopez saw the guard instead of Jacob, he rolled over to face the wall and remained silent. His duty fulfilled; Jacob went back to his room to mourn.

Jacob continued his new meal routine for days, choosing to let the guards serve the food, preventing him from doing more harm. He called Joan several times each day in a feeble attempt to close the chasm their daughter left in their lives. They took turns crying and consoling each other, finding only a microcosm of comfort in the calls.

It was on Sunday that the guard told him Lopez had refused to eat. "Tomorrow's his trial and we can't have him looking like his own people. He says he'll eat if you bring him dinner tonight."

Jacob let out a sigh and nodded.

"He also has one last request. The Brass would like you to consider it." the guard said.

"And that is?" Jacob asked.

"He wants you to play one last game." the guard nodded to the red and black checkers set by the door.

Jacob balanced the tray with one arm and grabbed the set with his other. "Only because I'll never have to do this again."

"Is that you Jacob?" Lopez called from his cot as the door opened.

"It's me Luis." Jacob walked in and placed the tray on the table, unable to make eye contact in his shame.

"Will you stay with me and play one more game?" Lopez asked.

"I will." Jacob wanted to be done with this as quickly as possible.

"Good." Lopez took the board from Jacob and began to set up the game. "I'm very sorry for what was said, Jacob. I hope you and your wife are…"

"Don't talk about her. Let's just play." Jacob sat on the opposite end of the cot and made his first move.

"I need you to understand something." Lopez choked on his words and paused to gather his thoughts. "I am not a good man. I once was, and all I wanted was to help my people. But I found that wanting to do something, and being able to do something are two very different matters."

"Yes Luis, they are." Jacob sacrificed a piece to set up Lopez for a bigger loss.

Lopez moved his piece into Jacob's trap and let his hand linger for a moment over the board. "Every monster begins somewhere. My beginning was with the loss of my wife and granddaughter. You know how I lost them, no?"

Jacob blinked to focus his eyes back on Lopez. "No, I don't."

Lopez's voice lowered to almost a whisper. "I was working to rid my country of the corruption that had gripped it for decades. When I finally backed them into a corner, they did what all animals do when trapped. While my beloved filled their bags with clothes and baubles, my enemies filled their bodies with bullets. That day taught me that the only way to defeat your enemies is to become them."

Lopez looked back at the board and absently moved a

piece from his back row and looked up at Jacob. "I don't want your beginning as a monster to start with your daughter. I hope it doesn't start with me."

Jacob recoiled back. Lopez stared at him with wet eyes. "Please Jacob. Let me be the monster, and you can be the king."

Lopez had positioned his pieces in a sacrificial way. Jacob could jump several of them in one move, leaving his piece on the back row, kinged.

"I'm sorry Luis, I had no idea." Jacob said.

Lopez reached for Jacob and embraced him before he could pull away. Jacob let the man's arms envelop him, warm him, strengthen him from the weakness he felt. After a moment Lopez finally whispered, "No Jacob. Thank you for making this old monster feel like a man again."

Jacob sat in the country's highest court and watched the trial unfold. The coalition presented evidence of Lopez's war crimes, including the use of chemical weapons to wipe out an entire city block. The people of Uruguay sat as judge and jury, and with a quick verdict, his executioner.

As per Lopez's own laws, he was found guilty of crimes against the State. His punishment was death by firing squad, and it was to be performed immediately following the trial. Jacob watched as Lopez was blindfolded and led to the court-yard for execution. Monitors set up in the courtroom came to life as the countdown began, and without a final word, Lopez was killed by ten gunmen.

"One less monster in the world, and somehow, one less good man." Jacob said before offering a prayer for the dead.

TIM HEARE (Salt City Genre Writers) is always thinking of stories. Tim has a passion for learning about the world around him and uses his unique way of thinking to approach problems, find solutions, and create narratives that convey meaning about the human experience.

Tim holds a Bachelor's degree in Marketing from Utah State University and is a member of Mensa. He uses his knowledge of story and structure to align sales and marketing teams with customer expectations and needs that drive business for some of the world's biggest brands.

Tim enjoys experiencing any story, in any medium, that transports the audience into new worlds. He is passionate about comic books, Lego, stories, and of course, his family.

His first published work, *Amnesia and Other Short Stories*, can be found on Amazon. You can find him on LinkedIn and Medium @1genxer.

Liberty's Box

Jayrod P. Garrett

I. Trapped

This was my box. So small it never fit.
All to make certain I was seen, not heard.

Inside, I went to school and church where boys
chased me. Dad told me that was most important.

At home, Mom put on make-up for Daddy.
She showed me pretty was most important.

At church, my leaders told me to keep myself pure.
Chastity was most important.

So I teased the boys, made myself pretty,
and studied to understand purity.

II. Cut

It was not enough. At school they told me
to dance with a groping boy. I said no.

They said I can't say no. It might hurt him.
He raped me. I rushed home and washed myself

clean, pretty, and pure. It wasn't enough.
Father said I had to be to be desirable.

So I told my Bishop I wanted peace.
When I went back to school, I studied hard.

I graduated as the English Sterling Scholar.
And I applied to college–

but a boy stopped me. He courted me.
Married me for my purity, beauty, and voice.

III. Seeds

My box was full. Children, husband, and pets
left no room for me. And I still grew.

And I didn't know how to stop growing.
So I made a garden. And in that box I grew

peas, melons, sage, and thyme all fertilized
with the cuttings of myself that didn't fit.

It didn't hurt anymore, I told myself.
Except I cried myself to sleep most nights.

At church they told me "Women submit to your
husbands."
My husband said that's bullshit.

He said it keeps me in the God damn garden.
And he asked me to stop. I said no.

That night I buried his ring in the dirt.
I wasn't about to give up my freedom.

IV. Show and Tell

My daughter came to my garden.

She saw my blood in the dirt and asked what I
gave up tonight. I shivered realizing I didn't know.

I had her fetch Daddy and her brothers.
And I showed them everything I cut away
from dreams to bones to heart and soul.

I confessed about
wanting to go to college,
pursue politics, and travel to
the Great Wall of China.

She asked me why the Great Wall.
I said I wanted to know

if China cut themselves off
because they wanted to be smaller
or to keep themselves safe.

And I looked around
at my garden of desolation
where I buried my dreams,
tore out my heart, and slew my soul
I knew it was neither.
Walls, like knives, are weapons.

V. Becoming me

My husband asked
what do you want to grow here?
And I didn't know. I'd always
done what would nourish others.
I'd never thought about: What will nourish me?

And I ripped out the melons,
the peas, the sage and thyme, leaving
the ground bare but for the parts
of me that remained.
What I want and need.

I haven't gone to church since.
Instead I walked the Great Wall
and I learned Mandarin in College.
And French, Italian, and Swahili.
I've found work as a linguist.
I paid for my family to climb the Eiffel Tower,
visit the Leaning Tower of Pisa,
and this summer's trip traveling Tanzania.

My daughter keeps asking me
if I'm going to become the next Michelle Obama.
I laugh because she's the one who studied
political science and law, not me.

And these days I'm content with my studies
as I settle into the grassy knoll
with a maple tree that grew
in my garden. Here I've taught my children,
especially my daughter,
about Maya Angelou, Nora Jemisin, and Rosa Parks.
About how they chose to live,
the infinite worth of my children's lives,
and the comfort of choosing my own.

JAYROD P. GARRETT (Salt City Scribes, Salt City Genre
Writers) is a performance poet and storyteller from Ogden,
Utah. As a Black man living in Utah, he's long felt alone in a
culture that demanded his assimilation for survival. This is one
of the reasons he went to Weber State University to get his
degree in English to develop his own voice that he could be his
own person. In an effort to share what he learned there he
spent four years running an open mic in Ogden called Voices.
Inspired by current events he's engaged in a new project
developing Utah's first Black Artist Collective while working on
his first novel. He lives in Bountiful with his wife Melissa and
their two sons. You can find his poetry and blogs at:
jayrodpgarrett.com.

POETS' SESSION SUNDAY FEATURE OF CONFERENCE

Round-up Aides

Mrs. Dave Wangsgaard To Greet Writers At Breakfast

The program for the poets' breakfast, which will be the Sunday morning feature of the League of Utah Writers two-day round-up here, August 10-11, will be as follows:

Greetings, by Mrs. Dave Wangsgaard, chairman; introduction of Maude Blixtrone, Salt Lake City poet, toastmistress. The guest of honor will be Edith Cherrington, Pasadena, Calif., poet, formerly of Marysvale, Utah, who will present the awards of the poetry contest which she sponsored. The awards will be copies of her book, "Poems Editors Buy," for the first two prizes, and a third prize, "Down This Road," by Mrs. Dave Wangsgaard.

The program will be: Solo by George Frost, accompanied by Lester Hinchliff. "Where Is Sylvia"; poems, which will be read by the following: Celia VanCott, Blanche Kendall McKey's poem which will be read by Ruth Thatcher; Lou Larsen, Veneta Nielsen, Ivy Williams Stone, LaMont Johnson, Olive McHugh, Olive Woolley Burt, Carlton Culmsee, Marge Stewart, Ed Tuttle, Cleone Montgomery, Claire Stewart Boyer, Lawrence J. Sorenson, Ivy Houtz Woolley, Anna Prince Redd, and former Governor Charles R. Mabey, Lucile Iredale Carleson, Radcliff Squires, Vesta Cherrington, Wyroa Hansen, Hortense Spencer Andersen, Christie Lund, Eva Willis Wangsgaard.

The program will conclude with a trio number, selections from Milton's "Lost Paradise," under the direction of Mr. Hinchliff.

EVA WILLES WANGSGAARD
... Breakfast chairman

ERNEST A. LAWRENCE
... He's free-lance writer

The Ogden Standard-Examiner | August 9, 1940

Freedom Comin'

Denis Feehan

They wrapped him tight in iron chains
And threw him in a wooden boat
With fifty other starving blacks
And a hundred well fed goats

They marched him down to Massa's house
A giant home of wood and brick
But *he* would get a broken shack
Near the cotton fields he'd pick

He worked the fields from dawn to dusk
To make his quota every day
'Cause boss man whipped a boy who slacked
And the hounds bit runaways

They took away his language
And made him learn their English some
They forced their Christianity
On his babies, now they come

They tore those screaming kids
From their weeping mama's arms
And then shipped those boys to far-off farms

The farms they took those children to
Put chains and rags on everyone
A century or two would pass
Till their freedom could be won

Some four score after whites were freed
The president removed the chains
And men who bled at boss man's whim
Now had freedom in their veins

But freedom is a fleeting thing
And angry men in pointed hoods
Took simple men from tiny farms
And then hanged 'em in the woods

And ol' Jim Crow said no, no, no
You ride the bus, you sit in back
You walk our streets, you step aside
Yeah you're free but you're still black

The lynchings soon began
And the papers showed the sights
In a photograph of smiling Knights.

Then Rosa Parks refused to stand
And thousands followed MLK
Across a bridge that gave them hope
They would overcome some day

The music world was the first to fall
As blues morphed into Rock N Roll
The record stores dropped Doris Day
And the whites bought Motown Soul

The TV sets in every house
Showed athletes of a different hue
Like Wilt the Stilt and ol' James Brown
Jackie R. in Dodger blue

A black man ran for Senator
Continuing their social climb
Pointed hats and Nazi brats
Couldn't stop the march of time

In late O-Eight the country watched
A black man lead the way
From whips & chains and cotton fields
To a brand-new hopeful day

FREEDOM COMIN', Y'ALL, FREEDOM COMIN'

DENIS FEEHAN (Heritage Writers Guild President) has been
published in three different anthologies and has pieces in two
new anthologies this year. He is also the keyboard player in a
classic rock band and an actor and director for the Mesquite
Community Theater.

Club Members Continue to Hold Meetings
As Calendar Brings Formal Season Near

PRICE—Accepted at the recent Writers' round-up as a chapter of the League of Utah Writers, the Price club was designated as Southeastern League of Utah Writers.

Five charter members who qualified for membership are Lamont Johnson of Huntington; Mrs. Molly M. Schultz of Latuda, club president; Mrs. Jeanet M. Barker, Mrs. Leola S. Anderson and H. Duane Anderson, all of Price.

The club will meet with associate members Sunday at 5 p. m. at the Helper library, where Mrs. Schultz, Mr. Johnson and Mrs. Ethel Dubois will report the activities of the round-up.

Sunday Morning Breakfast club members were guests at the home of Mr. and Mrs. Karl M. Jameson this week. Present were Mr. and Mrs. Hal G. McKnight, Mr. and Mrs. George B. Wallace and Mr. and Mrs. J. Garth Hall.

Entre Nous club members were entertained by Mrs. Maurice Tatton Thursday evening with bridge following dainty refreshments. The event honored Mrs. M. D. Jones, whose birthday falls in this month. As is the custom of the club, the honored guest

Country Club

was complimented w shower.

There were three guests.

Guests of Mrs. Nic members of the Tu were entertained at bridge. Twelve gu seated at tables beau tered with purple petunias.

A feature of the en was introduced in a cool" idea, appropri occasion.

A lawn party greet clubwomen at the h Eunice Tucker last Sweetpeas formed th table decoration, an

The Salt Lake Tribune | August 18, 1940

Away

Cassidy Ward

"Y ou still in the kitchen, Maxey?" Charger yelled from his permanent crater in the couch of the upstairs living room.

Charger's bond with that couch could be described in chemical terms; if scientists had known to look in this room they might have unlocked the secret to stable fusion power. His relationship with Max, however, was decaying like francium covered in maggots.

She hated being called Maxy, or Maxine, or Maximilian, and he knew it. So, when she didn't answer, he tried once more, this time with the proper title.

"Max … grab me the Cheetos before you come back up, will ya?"

What Charger didn't know was that Max hadn't been in the kitchen at all; she had been standing in front of the door with a full backpack and her hand on the knob, gathering the courage to leave. Courage that, just a moment before, she had found.

He hadn't heard the door creak open, or the way she softly closed it on her way out, and he didn't hear the tears she had stifled behind the crux of her elbow. He wouldn't notice for several more minutes that she had gone. And by then, all of his searching and screaming and wanting would be too late.

She walked with determination down the dimly lit sidewalk. She wasn't running, at least not outside of her mind, but she wasn't staying, either. Not anymore.

She travelled on foot for several blocks through the town where they had built a life. The car was in his name, almost everything was. There was very little in the world that she owned that wasn't now perched upon her back.

Each building, each street sign, each passing corner brought with it a memory of time spent with the man she once loved, the man she maybe still loved, but couldn't be around any longer.

She had tried to tell him how he was stifling her, how his tiny aggressions had eroded her soul like the waves against the shore, how she needed to get away from this town, from that house, from the permanent residence he had taken up on their couch. His couch.

She had tried half a hundred times but could never get the words to come out right. Or, if she did, he didn't hear her. So in the end she packed her bag, left him a note of apology, or maybe just explanation, and left.

She imagined him in the house, calling to her, wondering where she was. She imagined him reading the note, tears falling from his cheeks, intermingling with the ones she had left on that single page. She imagined the heartbreak she was causing him, she could feel it mirrored by her very own, but she didn't cry. Max didn't shed a single tear now, because for the first time in a long time, that heartbreak she had felt for as long as she could remember had taken a back seat to an overwhelming feeling of freedom.

Thunder rumbled overhead and a light spattering of rain began. The familiar wet scent engulfed her and she kept walking. Slowly, strip malls and corner grocers gave way to ramshackle ramblers and hayfields. The sounds of town, that neverending background noise, so consistent you forget that it's there, faded away. Max felt the silence pressing down on her, broken only by the staccato beat of the rain against the ground.

Eventually, even the teetering barns disappeared until all that was left was alfalfa, swaying in the wind, and trees in the distance.

She didn't quite know where she was going and she didn't much care. Away was her only destination and with each soggy step through the dirt and the brush she got closer to wherever that was.

At first, she didn't notice the buzzing in her pocket. The thrumming of the rain and her constant footfalls over pavement drowned it out. In the midst of her wandering she hadn't stopped to consider that he would call, that anyone would call.

A small boulder, just off the trail, made a worthy enough perch. She sat, ungloved her right hand and thrust it into her pocket to retrieve the phone.

She had three missed calls and he was calling again. Max sat for a moment just looking at the screen. The flashing contact information with the photo of them together outside a movie theater growing ever more obscured by the fat raindrops that were by now falling, like the broken pieces of her previous life, from the sky. She hadn't meant to bring the phone, she didn't think she'd need it. She hadn't even brought a charger, purposely left it home, plugged into the wall outlet above the kitchen counter.

Max almost answered, but found her resolve. She stood from her seat on the boulder, set her phone into a crook in the stone, readjusted the pack on her back and walked away, cutting the final tie from the life that had imprisoned her.

She could hear the buzzing growing fainter and eventually

melting into the sound of the rain as she walked toward the trees ahead.

In her pack, she had a few changes of clothes, enough food for a week—if she rationed or found vegetation or game with which to supplement, a small tent, a smaller blanket, a tarp, three empty water bottles, and a few books; H.G. Wells, Jules Verne, J.M. Barrie.

Her intent was to spend a few days in the woods, dream of high adventure, and gather her thoughts. She had no plan for what would come next. In fact, having no plan was her plan.

A small clearing in the woods made for a fine place to set up camp; the canopy held off most of the rain. Max set her tent at the base of a large tree, using its thick trunk for extra bracing and the leaves for covering.

She opened the three empty bottles, placing a filtration tablet inside each one and tied the tarp between two branches to catch rainwater.

The rain increased in ferocity with each passing moment. As the downpour reached its peak, the canopy stopped being any help. Max struggled to set up the tent in the rain. The canvas was slick and uncooperative.

She found herself wondering if she'd made a mistake. Was she escaping a toxic situation or just running away from her problems? Still, she persisted and eventually the tent was ready.

Once under the protection of the canvas and out of the rain, her doubts melted away, and she set to unpacking her things.

By the time she was done, the tarp was heavy with water. Max filled the three bottles and screwed on the caps, wiped them down, and returned two of them to her pack.

Max huddled in the opening of her tent, wrapped in the thin blanket, sipping rain water, and cracked open the first novel that reached her hand. She didn't care which one; she loved them all, knew them all, wanted nothing more than to inhabit any one of them, to break off the concrete shoes of ordinary life and be somewhere else. Be someone else.

Night was falling over the world drowning out what little light wasn't already swallowed by the clouds and tree cover. She almost regretted leaving the phone back on that boulder beyond the forest, if only for the light.

Max considered going back for it but had doubts that it would still work after an hour or more in the downpour. She didn't know exactly how long it had been; she hadn't brought a watch either, so she did her best to read the words in the diminishing light, filling in what she couldn't see with the details ingrained in her memory. But before long it was simply too dark to go on and she placed the book back into her pack for safe keeping.

Finally, the rain drizzled out and was replaced by almost total darkness and the music of insects coming out to greet the earth renewed. The chirping of crickets and cicadas seemed to be singing her name and she couldn't sleep. So, with a fistfull of jerky and a fresh bottle of water she set out to greet them in return, leaving the half-emptied bottle out in the night to gather drops from the leaves.

Her pace was slow and steady, testing the ground with each step. Beyond the small and lonely valley where she left all of her earthly belongings, the trees were sparser and the stars were beginning to shine through the leaves, allowing for just enough light by which to navigate, however treacherously.

Occasionally a twig would snap beneath her boot heel and the song of the wood would pause for a moment before beginning again with renewed intensity.

She took special care to make note of certain landmarks, creating a mental map to find her way back; large cracked stone, dead tree, snake hole, and so on. She sang them back to herself in reverse, adding the newest ones to the front of the list.

Max had just taken note of a bleached deer skull gleaming alabaster against the dirt when she fell.

Distracted, she hadn't noticed the tangled branch that caught her foot and sent her tumbling down a steep incline. In that frozen moment even the insects paused, as if holding their breath.

She came to a stop with a sudden thud and a sharp inhalation and lay in the velvety moss trying to capture her breath.

She was alive and mostly uninjured. The cicadas let out a sigh of relief and she could hear them again through the ringing in her ears. It was another moment before she noticed that the ambient glow around her wasn't coming from the stars, but from a large metal object beside her.

She spent several moments just staring, her mind unwilling to take in what she was seeing. It was approximately twelve feet long from end to end and tall enough to stand inside. It was ovular in shape, save that one end was tapered, like an egg stretched out and tipped on its side.

Max stood abruptly, wincing at her aching joints and bruised frame. She took a long, hard look at the shimmering object, with its glowing and its thrumming, then back up at the steep gradient.

The object looked otherworldly, yet somehow inviting, and the incline looked arduous even without minor injuries, but at least it was familiar.

Instinct, of course, told her to climb as fast and as far as she could. Her camp, she estimated, was a good half mile away after the climb back to the top of the hill; the bleached skull; then the snake hole; the dead tree; and the cracked stone. But there she would find a blanket and her books, and some sense of familiarity.

Another part of her, the part she had kept buried for so long, was screaming at her to investigate the situation in which she now found herself.

Then she asked herself a simple question, one she had been asking since she was a girl but had never given the proper weight: What would Phileas Fogg do? What would the time traveler or Griffin do? What would Pan do? And she took her first tentative steps toward the shimmering object, iridescent in the starlight.

Max approached slowly, both in an attempt to minimize the pain in her ankles and to gain the courage needed to move forward. What could the object be? she wondered. Upon first inspection there seemed to be no creases, no opening, no defining characteristics save for the shape, the glow, and the low thrum.

Mustering all of her courage she repeated a mantra in her mind, *Fogg, the traveler, Griffin, Pan*, and placed a hand on the object, tracing its side from left to right.

Max completed a full circle, arriving back at the point where she'd started and discovered ... nothing.

She stood there hobbling, shifting weight from one foot to the other for a moment, then glanced back toward the hill and the hike she would have to make on wounded feet to get back to her camp, then took a step away from the object.

The insects looked on from their many varied posts and began to sing tenfold, then stopped abruptly. The forest fell completely silent. There were no more rain drops, no more forest songs, no more thrumming, but there was light.

Max turned back toward the object to see that it had changed slightly in shape and structure, an opening was now visible directly in front of her and inside she could see a corridor that widened at the end. The interior of the object appeared as heated metal, shifting in color, smooth and almost featureless.

The ambient blue light that had previously filled the clearing came shining through brighter and fuller than before. It bled through the translucent metal and spilled onto the forest floor. Now, no longer obscured by the object's exterior, it filled the immediate area in artificial daylight.

Fogg, the traveler...

She stepped toward the object once more, this time entering through the opening in its side. The corridor was narrow, but wide enough to move through unimpeded. Once inside she could see two smaller compartments toward the rounded end, separated by a wall but identical in layout, and one larger room toward the point. She moved toward the tapered end, keeping one eye on the doorway.

The corridor opened into a moderately sized room. In the center was a chair, or what looked like a chair. As best as Max could tell, the chair floated with no attachment either above or below, as though it had frozen in the moment of falling.

The rest of the room was empty. Facing forward, Max could see through the pointed end out into the forest, the metal acting like one way glass or some highly advanced display screen, taking the images from outside and projecting them on the walls.

The adrenaline of the fall and of her discovery started to wane and her bruised and tweaked frame began demanding more attention. She took a seat, if only to rest before she continued exploring.

"Hello, Maxine." A voice from somewhere within the object addressed her, it seemed to be coming from all around, from the object itself. It sounded human, but with a thrumming underneath, the same thrum she had heard in the forest outside. "You may call me Jophiel," it concluded.

She looked up, then to her left, her right, and behind. No one was there.

"Um, call me Max," she responded, not knowing what else to say.

"Very well Max, where would you like to go?"

"Go?" She responded.

"Yes, Max. I can take you anywhere you'd like to go."

Max gasped when the image outside shifted as Jophiel lifted away from the ground to hover just above the forest canopy. From this vantage point, Max could see the trees stretching out into the darkness. She could see the short path back to the city and the life she'd left behind. And she could see the stars shining brightly up ahead. A vast infinity, waiting.

"Anywhere?" she asked skeptically.

"Yes, anywhere but back."

She turned back, toward the corridor, and saw that the door had closed. A momentary sense of panic seized her. She was trapped. Then a calm fell over her as she realized that she was only trapped if she wanted to leave. And she didn't want to leave.

Still, Max didn't understand. She shook her head, just slightly. "Why me?"

For a lingering moment the ship didn't answer, even the thrumming diminished until it was barely audible. And then—

"I was once like you. Full of potential. Full of dreams. But trapped."

Max traced her thumb along the right hand rest and felt an imperfection. A deep gouge. Only then did she see Jophiel truly. Every wall, every console, every surface was littered with dents and dings, with deep cuts.

"What happened? Who did this?"

Another pause.

"That matters not. What matters is this moment. I am free. And now, so are you."

"What about my things? My tent, my blanket …" she asked, mostly to herself.

"I will provide you with everything you need," Jophiel responded.

"My stories?"

Fogg, the traveler, Griffin, Pan … she thought to herself one final time. In the end she decided she didn't need them anymore; she would make her own.

"Jophiel, take me away."

CASSIDY WARD (Salt City Genre Writers) is an award winning author of short stories, and a journalist covering science and pop culture. His stories have been published in anthologies including *A Little Wrong* and *By Virtue Fall*, as well as *One Mean Monster Zine*. His journalism can be found at outlets like SYFY.com, Observer.com, and StarTrek.com. You can find his shortest writings (courtesy of character limits) on Twitter at @CassidyWard.

Twelve

Rachael Bush

One day, half of my family left.

I heard my mother say her divorce from my dad was messy. For her, I'm sure it was. But for us, it was chaotic. Somehow, the silence of separation was worse than the screaming matches.

My brother and I were devastated. Our sister got to pick. She chose our dad. We would've chosen him too, but we were too young. I have no idea who chose the arbitrary age when children have a voice in court, but in Utah in the eighties, it was twelve. Our sister was sixteen. Definitely old enough to be recognized by the courts. I was eight and my brother was ten, so we were assets awarded to our mother.

Floral couch. Check.

Heirloom china. Check.

Voiceless children. Check.

We moved away from the life we knew to another state where one of our mother's boyfriends was waiting. They married soon after.

Consumed by anger and grief, I hid from everyone for the

first year. By the second year, I came out of my shell a little. I wish I hadn't.

Discipline had always been doled out by our mother. The belt was her weapon of choice. But our mother's new husband took over at bedtime. He liked to hurt me and my brother. Not in the same way, because we weren't at all alike. My brother was loud and brave and confrontational. He got hit. Slapped. Choked. Punched. I was meek and quiet and obedient. I was touched. Caressed. Restrained. Invaded. He was eleven. I was nine.

Unified against the monster we lived with, the abuse brought my brother and me together. Eventually, we told our mother. She laughed and said my brother deserved it. He was too mouthy and needed to learn his place. She rolled her eyes at me and said I was overreacting and needed to learn how to enjoy getting a massage.

We should've told our dad, but we didn't. Not at first. It was too scary. What if he didn't believe us either? By keeping it to ourselves, we could pretend we had someone looking out for us. Someone who could potentially be on our side. Clinging to that last hope kept us going. Besides, it wouldn't have changed anything. Until we had a legal voice, we had to do whatever we could to survive.

My brother's plan was to draw attention away from me. He picked fights to spare me, and there was nothing I could do but listen to the sounds of the struggle and cry into my pillow. When I tried to help, we would both get hurt, and that defeated the purpose of the plan.

The closer it got to his twelfth birthday, the more anxious I became. He almost had his freedom. It was a day of celebration and dread.

I assumed he would jump at the chance to get away, but when it finally arrived, he didn't go. He told me he couldn't leave me. We both knew why.

He paid dearly to protect me for the next two years.

Inspired by his sacrifice and bravery, I eventually found my voice. I learned to say no when I was eleven. I screamed and kicked and thrashed. I carried around my anger and unleashed it when I needed to. Turned off by my wild behavior, our mother's husband lost interest.

My brother and I counted down the days to my twelfth birthday, and when our day in court finally arrived, we went together and told the truth.

The judge asked why my brother didn't leave when he had the chance if things were really as bad as we said they were. With my hand in his, he said he wouldn't leave until we were both free.

That was the day I got the other half of my family back. We couldn't go back to the life we had, so we started an even better one.

RACHAEL BUSH (Blue Quill) published her fourth book, *Love on Location*, with The Wild Rose Press in 2018 under her pen name, September Roberts. As September, she writes romance that's smoking hot and always happy ever after. As Rachael, she writes short stories about her tumultuous childhood and the *Botany for Everyone* series. When she's not writing, she volunteers for the League of Utah Writers as the Blue Quill chapter president, the Marketing Chair, and builds the app for our conferences. For nerdy science and art, follow Rachael on Instagram @botanyforeveryone.

Arranges Writers' Round-Up

Mrs. Larry P. Wright, of Ogden, president of the Blue Quill chapter, League of Utah Writers, and chairman of the fifth annual Utah Writers' Round-Up, which will be held in Ogden August 10 and 11.

Chairman Invites Scribes To Ogden Conference

Tribune Intermountain Wire

OGDEN—Writing to writers is a special kind of adventure, according to Mrs. Larry P. Wright of Ogden, president of the Blue Quill chapter, League of Utah Writers and chairman of the fifth annual Utah Writers' Round-Up.

In this latter capacity, Mrs. Wright has contacted notable writers of the entire west, and their letters concerning the round-up, their interest in the project and their present activities have been even more fascinating than their published works, Mrs. Wright said.

The round-up, which will be held August 10 and 11 at the Hotel Ben Lomond in Ogden, is in the hands of a committee headed by Mrs. Wright.

The program will include meetings on Saturday from 10 a. m. to noon and from 2:45 to 5:30 p. m. and on Sunday from 2 to 5 p. m. Luncheon Saturday at 12:30 p. m.; open house Saturday evening, and the poets' breakfast Sunday at 10:30 a. m., are all included in the reservation fee.

Reservations may be made with Mrs. Anderson in Ogden, with Mrs. W. Ray Montgomery in Salt Lake City; with Mrs. H. M. Redd in Provo or Mrs. Gomer Peacock in Price.

Writers Arrange Poetry Contest

A poetry contest for all Utahns was announced Wednesday by Mrs. W. E. Tangren, secretary of the Salt Lake chapter, League of Utah Writers. The contest, which will be judged in connection with the fifth annual Utah Writers' Round-Up in Ogden, August 10 and 11, is limited to verse of not more than 32 lines, either published or unpublished. Mrs. Edith Cherrington, nationally known poet and author of the book, "Poems Editors Buy," who will be a speaker at the Round-Up, will judge the contest.

First prize will be a copy of Mrs. Cherrington's book and second prize will be a copy of Eva Willes Wangsgard's new volume of poetry, "Down This Road."

Entries must be mailed to Mrs. Tangren before August 7.

The Salt Lake Tribune | August 1, 1940

Hippocrates

Bryan Young

J ean-Pierre sipped his wine. What else could he do while
Nazis rifled through his barn but drink?

"They are still searching?" came a harsh, worried
whisper from below the floorboards.

"*Oui*. They are leaving no stone unturned. It is good we
moved you here last night."

"They will find our things—"

"We hid them well."

"What if they search the house?"

Jean-Pierre dabbed at his forehead with a handkerchief.
Nervous. "Remain quiet and they won't."

The Free French fighter beneath his feet, one of three, shut
her mouth. Of course she did; what else could she do?

Jean-Pierre took another sip of his wine, hoping it would
calm his nerves. He might have been a very bad doctor and an
even worse freedom fighter, but at least he was a good drunk.
"They are coming out of the barn now."

"How many are there?"

"Shhh," Jean-Pierre said. "There are only two—a captain
and the one doing the work. He looks no older than seventeen.

Is that how bad this has gotten? They're sending children now?"

"It was always this bad," Monette said.

"Shhh!" Jean-Pierre said, louder. "The boy is bleeding. He must have hurt himself. They're coming toward the house. Why did you all get me involved in this? I am a coward. Now keep your tongues quiet."

"You volunteered," she reminded him. "You said you wanted to help."

Her voice was the last sound Jean-Pierre heard before the loud and brutal knock at his front door. He drained the rest of the deep burgundy from his glass, hoping it would bolster and fortify him.

Jean-Pierre thought it best not to keep the fascists waiting and, since he had a part to play, shuffled to the door like a good goose-stepping supporter. He opened the door wide, relaxed his shoulders, trying not to look down on them or look suspicious in any way. He couldn't tell if smiling would give him away as being a fraud or put them at ease. He wasn't very good at smiling anyway, so he kept his face mute.

"Can I help you—" Jean-Pierre looked to the soldier's collar to realize he wasn't really a captain. "—Sergeant?"

The sergeant's eyes narrowed. "Strasser. Sergeant Strasser."

"Yes, of course, Sergeant Strasser. How can I be of assistance?"

"You are a doctor, yes?"

"Yes, I am."

Sergeant Strasser looked down at the corporal's bloodied hands, the wound on his left hand covered with his right palm to stop the bleeding.

"Oh, yes, of course. Come in, please."

The last thing Jean-Pierre wanted to do was invite a pair of Nazis into his home, but he had little choice. They had guns and bad dispositions. Also they were fascists and wanted good people dead and did what they wanted no matter what. He wanted to be left to harbor their enemies in peace, but they kicked in every door and lit every peaceful place ablaze. What good was "superiority" if you couldn't use it to relax?

"Sit, sit here." Jean-Pierre directed the young corporal to the heavy oak dining table and sat him down near the end. "If you will excuse me, I'll just get my medical bag."

The sergeant never sat. He followed Jean-Pierre into the next room, keeping his hands clasped neatly behind his back the entire time. Likely to ensure that Jean-Pierre fetched his bag and not a gun. Nazis were, to Jean-Pierre's mind, a cowardly and superstitious lot. The medical bag wasn't far, so the Nazi didn't follow for very long. It was on the counter just inside of the kitchen.

Jean-Pierre wondered if he *should* have kept a gun in his medical bag. Somehow, that would have felt wrong given his oath. He was a bad doctor, sure, but he had his ideals and the weight of swearing to do no harm bearing down on him.

Couldn't Nazis be different, though? Like fighting an infection? A doctor didn't bother to save the bacteria that threatened to turn a wound gangrenous; their oath covered no such things. Why would it be different with Nazis and the infection they represented, giving the world itself necrotic rot?

Jean-Pierre shrugged as he snatched his bag and a clean dish towel. He marched back to the front room and sat alongside the too-young corporal, laying the towel out on the table and gently lifting the boy's hand onto it.

"Now let me take a look at this," he said, trying to focus on the fact that he'd be sewing up a wound, rather than thinking about the three Free French fighters waiting silently beneath his floorboards.

Sewing up a Nazi was the price to be paid in this instance to do no harm.

The sergeant circled the room as though he were conducting a barracks inspection. He took careful note of every book and knickknack on Jean-Pierre's shelf as he spoke. "So, *Herr Doktor*, it is known that you live here alone and tend to the village?"

"And the animals, yes," Jean-Pierre said, trying to ignore the sergeant's search. The laceration along the side of the corporal's hand cut deep and would definitely require stitches. Putting on his best bedside manner, he looked up warmly at the corporal. "How did you do this, Corporal?"

"In the barn. The thresher."

"Ah, dangerous things, those. Let me see what I can do about this. I'll get some water. We shall clean the wound, and I shall sew it. Hold the towel down on it, though. Apply firm pressure, and we'll see if we can slow the bleeding"

"*Danke.*" The corporal folded the towel over the wound and gripped it tightly, staining everything crimson.

The sergeant turned back to the table and watched Jean-Pierre stand with the accusing glare of a suspicious police detective.

"If you will excuse me a moment, Sergeant, I will grab a bowl of water, and we'll straighten your young charge out."

Jean-Pierre made his way to the kitchen, and the sergeant followed. Jean-Pierre fetched a wooden bowl from the cupboard and rolled his sleeves up before turning on the faucet.

"How long have you lived here?" the sergeant asked.

"Since '35 or so."

"By yourself?"

"Since my wife died, yes."

"A lonely life?"

As Jean-Pierre filled the bowl with warm water, he shrugged. "Peaceful. For the most part, the war has passed me by. I work the field; I stitch the occasional cut. I birth calves now, or did when there were cows, which is something I never would have guessed I'd do in my days in Paris. I have plenty of time to drink these days."

"Paris is a lovely city. Were you here when we took it?"

"Indeed," Jean-Pierre said. He knew bait when he saw it. The sergeant wanted to goad him into a debate to see where his loyalties might be. But what could he say that wouldn't arouse suspicion?

Instead of responding further, Jean-Pierre moved past the sergeant and brought the bowl to the table beside the corporal.

"I was there that day," the sergeant said, not leaving the kitchen. "We threw a parade."

"I'm sure."

Jean-Pierre wiped his brow with his forearm and sat next to the corporal who may have just graduated the Hitler Youth a week prior. The doctor took in a deep breath and eyed the shadow of the Nazi in the kitchen. He needed to bring him back into the front room. Yes, a carpet covered the trapdoor in the kitchen that led to the root cellar, but any wrong move or noise would doom them all. Jean-Pierre remembered the weapons the partisans brought with them. No doubt they clutched the old rifles and pistols, ready to fire.

No. Not a single one of them would leave his home alive if he didn't stop the Nazis from searching too thoroughly.

"What did you think when you heard the news?" the sergeant asked. The squeak of a cabinet door opening told Jean-Pierre that he was taking a deeper look in the kitchen.

"I'm an old man," Jean-Pierre said, loud enough for the sergeant to hear as he readied his needle and thread for the stitches. "War and revolution are games for the young. I will take what comes."

"A wise foreign policy."

"I'm Swiss at heart. My mother was Swiss, you know."

The corporal clenched his jaw when the doctor touched

the towel. Jean-Pierre knew the poor boy felt the pain of the slice. It really was quite deep.

"I know what you need," Jean-Pierre said to the boy. Then he raised his voice, "Sergeant, could I ask for your help? There is a wooden spoon in the drawer next to the sink. Could you bring it to me?"

The sergeant harrumphed, but the cabinet door closed. If nothing else, the search would end for a moment at least. Every second Jean-Pierre stalled was a second more of life he bought for those hidden downstairs. If he could buy an hour or a day or a week, he would do it. No matter the cost, it would be a small price to pay.

The sergeant arrived with the wooden spoon, and Jean-Pierre put on his warmest smile as he took it. "Now, Corporal, put this in your mouth and bite down hard. It won't take away the pain, but it will help."

The corporal took the spoon, his blood staining it red as he touched it, and put it between his teeth.

"There, there," Jean-Pierre said as he measured out the thread for the young man's wound. "I'll get through this as quickly as I can. Don't you worry. You'll be on your way before you know what happened."

"I appreciate your help, *Doktor*," the sergeant said. "Too often, the locals react in a way that requires . . . discipline."

"Can you blame them?" Jean-Pierre blurted it even before he realized what he'd done.

More than anything, he just wanted a drink.

The sergeant cocked an eyebrow. "Not at all. Caring for one's fatherland is admirable. But they should know by now that we are not going anywhere."

"As I said, I will take what comes." Jean-Pierre wished the wall the Nazis wanted to build, the one to keep everyone who didn't look like them out, could be built around them instead.

With all of the tools laid out, Jean-Pierre took a second

towel, dipped it into the warm water, and dabbed at the soldier's wound. He cleaned the blood from it and found the real edges of the laceration.

The corporal flinched with each probe of the wound.

"If you are not careful, this will become infected. When you get back to your base—or wherever it is that you report to your superiors—have them treat you with medicine that will prevent the infection."

"*Ja*," the boy said sloppily through the spoon, taking in sharp breaths as Jean-Pierre cleaned the wound even harder.

Jean-Pierre made no effort to be delicate. Though the corporal was just a boy, he *was* still a Nazi.

A foot shuffled somewhere below them.

Jean-Pierre remained a blank slate, focusing instead on thread. To mask the sound, he shifted his feet along the wooden floor and scooted his chair closer to the table.

If the sergeant noticed the sound as different than Jean-Pierre scooting across the floor, he made no indication. He turned from the shelf he'd been inspecting and looked back at the doctor and his patient.

"Where did you study to be a physician?" the Nazi asked.

"The *Sorbonne*." Jean-Pierre made a show of the hooked needle and turned to the boy. "This is going to hurt. I do apologize."

The boy nodded, bracing himself for the pain. To his credit, the corporal kept his arm still as he cringed, shutting his eyes tightly and biting down on the spoon with the verve of a starving wolf tearing into a deer carcass.

"So what is it you are looking for?" Jean-Pierre asked the sergeant as he made the first stab into the corporal's pink, Aryan skin, threading the first loop of the stitch.

The sergeant put down the vase on the entry table he'd taken to inspect. "Resistance."

"In the vase?"

"They leave signs."

"Do they make their way out here often?" Jean-Pierre looped the needle and thread through the skin on top of the boy's hand, making a tight stitch. Just because the boy was a Nazi didn't mean Jean-Pierre had to do bad work. "There seems very little to resist in the country."

The sergeant circled the room again, hands behind his back. "There is something to resist everywhere if you ask the right person."

When the Nazi made his way back toward the kitchen, toward the spot where the carpet hid the trapdoor, toward the partisans, Jean-Pierre's hand faltered with the next stitch.

The corporal whimpered, and the wooden spoon shifted in his mouth.

"I am so sorry," Jean-Pierre told the boy. "You'll have to keep your hand stiller than that, I'm sorry."

The sergeant paused, watching the exchange and eyeing the blood on his subordinate's uniform. "Have more dignity than that, Corporal. You'll already need a new uniform."

Jean-Pierre looped the hooked needle through the boy's skin once more and wondered what sort of organization would instill a disgust for human emotion. He sighed. It was the same organization that instilled a disgust for humans in general.

"A small price to pay," Jean-Pierre said. "One's life isn't worth a uniform."

Since he had to focus on the fine detail of the stitching, he couldn't keep track of the Nazi behind him. By the sound of his boot steps, the sergeant had made his way back into the kitchen for further inspection.

"Where is it that you are from, Sergeant?" Jean-Pierre said, loud enough to be heard in the other room.

Perhaps the sergeant didn't hear Jean-Pierre or perhaps he simply had no interest in responding. Worse still, what if the Nazi had found something? Was he crouched over the throw rug, lifting up its corners and seeing the seams of the door to the cellar beneath it?

All would be lost.

"Sergeant?" Jean-Pierre said, louder this time.

Jean-Pierre wondered what he would do if there were a scuffle, or if he would have to do something drastic. He looked up into the eyes of the frightened boy beneath his needle, bright blue saucers of fear. If a fight started, would there be any fight from him? Would Jean-Pierre need to tear the needle from the young soldier's hand and stab it into his throat while he wailed in pain?

Jean-Pierre wasn't sure he could do that.

He was much better at sewing people up than harming them, even Nazis. He was a doctor, not a butcher. And not even a very good doctor. A drunk doctor.

Jean-Pierre looped another stitch through the boy's skin.

Another noise from below.

Something dropped and hit the dirt floor.

Jean-Pierre couldn't help but react, glancing over at the boy. Luck held for Jean-Pierre as the boy's pain was too great to focus on the noise. But there was no guarantee the sergeant hadn't noticed.

"Did you hear that?" the sergeant said.

Jean-Pierre cleared his throat and slid his chair forward again, hoping the screech against the floor would add more plausible deniability to the increasing sounds from below.

Were they arguing? Were they holding André back from bursting through the floor and attacking? Or was it Claude?

Or was it simply a mouse?

There were field mice down there. Or rats.

Jean-Pierre hated that he had to make them sleep down there much of the time. He knew what that was like from the last war, sleeping in the dirt, covered in rats. He wished that no human would ever have to go through it again, but desperate times and all that . . .

"Sergeant?" he said again, louder. He wanted to just stand up and stop the sergeant. More than that, he wanted to stop time. Would that he could simply freeze everything and alter the landscape of his reality. But such things weren't possible. He had two more stitches to finish before he could stand and intercede, then he had to tie it off and cut the excess thread. He looped the thread through the corporal's skin again. "Just one more, son."

Both sides of the split in the boy's hand tightened together as he tugged on the string. Jean-Pierre couldn't hear the sergeant over the boy's whimpering as he tightened it, ready to tie the loop off.

He let his hands do the work they'd done a thousand times before. If he thought too hard about it, the muscle memories he'd built over the decades would get confused.

With the knot tied off and the edges clipped with his surgical scissors, he looked to the corporal. "You can take the spoon from your mouth now; it's over. I'll see if I can find some bandages to cover the wound."

"Danke."

Jean-Pierre tossed the tools into the bowl of water and bolted up from his chair, heading straight to the kitchen.

The sergeant crouched down low, reaching out for a corner of the obscuring carpet.

"He is almost done. I just need to get some bandages on his wound and you can be on your way." Jean-Pierre debated with himself about saying something else, something that might stand the sergeant back up, but attracting any more attention to his distractions would be a dead giveaway.

It didn't matter, though. The sergeant flipped the carpet over.

And there it was.

Plain as anything.

The seam in the floor and the inlaid handle to pull up the secret hatch. Revealed.

Instead of panicking, Jean-Pierre took a deep breath. "The wine cellar. Did you want some? A parting gift from me to you?"

The sergeant didn't even hear Jean-Pierre, nor his ruse to make the secret door unremarkable. Instead, he reached down for the metal handle, clinking as he pulled on it.

Jean-Pierre's eyes widened as the trapdoor burst open. A dark flash of a figure in a knit cap, likely André, burst from the door, knocking the Nazi onto his back.

A gun fired from the scuffle.

Jean-Pierre stood there, mouth agape, wondering about the growing pain in his middle. Reaching down brought nothing but pain in his gut. And moisture. He looked down to see blood all over his hands.

André leaped on top of the sergeant.

The corporal rushed into the room.

Another gun fired. Jean-Pierre couldn't tell if it was André's or the sergeant's. It didn't matter. Bullets had no nationalities.

All Jean-Pierre wanted was a drink.

The deep flavor of burgundy at the back of his tongue.

The courage that came with the deep red liquid.

Jean-Pierre collapsed onto his backside, trying desperately to stay upright, holding the counter with his free hand, clutching his stomach with the other. "Bon sang!"

The corporal used his good hand to pull André back by the scruff of his neck. Claude's head bobbed up from the floor, looking around, but the corporal booted him in the face.

"Claude," Jean-Pierre said, desperate, sinking deeper into the floor.

Another shot fired, and Jean-Pierre's hearing went. Like

he'd gone underwater. A ringing. A high-pitched squeal of a ring. A bacon-frying-on-a-pan sort of screech.

He looked up and saw the corporal's face, bleeding. A hole where his eye used to be, a spatter of red on the ceiling above him.

It didn't make sense.

The corporal collapsed, falling backward through the doorway to the front room.

Jean-Pierre watched Claude and Monette climb up from the cellar as André crawled onto the sergeant, keeping him wrestled to the ground.

"Go! Go!" André shouted at them. At least that's what it sounded like through the tinnitus. He could have been saying anything, really.

But it made sense when Claude and Monette made their break, stepping over the fallen corporal and fleeing the doctor's farmhouse.

Jean-Pierre tried to sit up, but the abdominal pain jolted him, a shocking bolt of fury that shot through his body. Dizziness took him. The blood drained from his face, through his body, all over the floor . . .

He rolled over, hoping that would make getting to his feet easier. He couldn't let things stop like this. He had to get up. To stand. For himself. For those in his care. For the cause.

Do no harm.

The ringing in his ears transformed to a tinny piano set to the tune of "La Marseillaise," and that inspired him up to his knees.

Then came the hard part.

André stood, extricating himself from the sergeant; he kicked the Nazi like he would a rabid dog and backed away. He tripped on the corporal's corpse but straightened himself on the doorjamb and sprinted away, out of Jean-Pierre's increasingly blurry field of view.

Jean-Pierre groaned and turned on his knees as the sergeant struggled to his feet. Steadying himself on the counter, the Nazi tightened his grip on his pistol and staggered past his subordinate's body.

Jean-Pierre lifted himself up, feeling like his bowels were spilling out of him and all of his blood gushed to the floor in one horrific cascade. He shambled forward, tightening the grip on the leak in his middle.

"What a waste," he wheezed as he stepped over the corporal, glancing at the poor boy's hand to see if the stitches had held despite his exertions. They had, and Jean-Pierre at least felt a pang of satisfaction about that.

In the front room, the sergeant stood at the door, aiming his pistol at the fleeing Free French.

"Non." Jean-Pierre staggered forward, one step at a time. If he wasn't careful, the sergeant was going to kill someone.

The gun fired.

Looking beyond the Nazi, Jean-Pierre watched André run. Beyond him were Claude and Monette. He didn't know if he had it in him to sew up another bullet hole for them; they *had* to escape in better health than he'd found them.

The Nazi fired again.

There was more to the pain in Jean-Pierre's stomach than the bullet. A sickness that came with understanding. Of knowing what he had to do if he wanted to help.

Jean-Pierre groaned in pain, from his heart more than his gut, and steadied himself on the table. He took a breath and snatched his scissors, sticking handles up in the bowl of bloodied water.

What was his name again? Strasser. Right. Sergeant Strasser fired once more. A puff of dirt erupted at André's feet.

Gripping the scissors, Jean-Pierre stepped forward, knowing what had to happen but still hoping it wouldn't.

The partisans had to get away.

The Nazis had to be stopped.

He wondered if they would remember him as a fool for thinking he could placate them or even heal them instead of resorting to violence first.

Jean-Pierre limped forward, and the gun fired once more. The roar of the ocean filled his ears, and he barely heard the hi-hat drum-hit of the gunshot. He watched the spent shell casing pop to the ground.

"It will be okay," Jean-Pierre said in his best bedside manner.

Jean-Pierre didn't know what a pair of sharp surgical scissors in the neck felt like, but he imagined it was roughly equal to the pain in his gut.

Blood spurted in the air, a crimson fountain.

There went his oath.

Strasser fired again, but at nothing in particular. The bullet splintered a hole into the wood of Jean-Pierre's porch.

Jean-Pierre withdrew the scissors from Strasser and wondered what his first name might be before plunging them into his neck again.

Strasser collapsed in a heap this time.

And Jean-Pierre followed.

His focus blurred. He thought he had blood in his eyes.

But he saw the three of them, the partisans he'd broken his oath to protect, escaping. Running to the trees. Vanishing among them.

"*Marchons,*" Jean-Pierre whispered in time to the music in his ears as his vision faded to black. "*Marchons . . .*"

BRYAN YOUNG (Salt City Genre Writers) is an award-winning author, filmmaker, and journalist who works in many different media. As a writer, he's had numerous novels and short stories published and has worked professionally in the Star Wars, Robotech, and BattleTech universes. His most recent novel is *BattleTech: Honor's Gauntlet.* He's written comics for Slave Labor Graphics and Image Comics and written and produced documentary films that were called "filmmaking gold" by the New York Times. As a journalist, he's had bylines at the Huffington Post, StarWars.Com, HowStuffWorks, /Film, Syfy, and many more. He's the president of the Salt City Genre Writers, a Salt Lake City-based chapter of the League of Utah Writers and also serves on the state board of that organization as Historian. He teaches writing for Writer's Digest and the University of Utah. You can learn more about him by following him on Twitter @swankmotron or by visiting his website, www.swankmotron.com.

What can the LUW do for you?

As a member of the League of Utah Writers, and now as a member of the Executive Committee for the past couple of years, I've been asked on several occasions what the League can do for people and why someone would want to join us. It turns out there are several answers, which means the best answer varies based on individual needs. The League of Utah Writers has a mission statement that can give us a little guidance here.

The League of Utah Writers is a non-profit organization dedicated to offering friendship, education, and encouragement to the writers and poets of Utah. Our organization aids our members in the improvement of their craft and support of their goals.

Picking out principles within the mission statement one at a time, I'll share what I've learned about the League and its benefits. First, there is friendship. I've made quite a few new friends because of the League, which is an amazing accomplishment for someone who would naturally hang back in the shadows. Most of my life, I've had only a few close friends, but the League has catapulted me into the midst of people with a wide range of backgrounds, but who share a common love of writing. That common interest has forged untold numbers of friendships between members over the years and will continue to do so.

Education is another huge aspect of the League. We have chapter meetings, Spring Conference, Quills Conference, and a host of other events and opportunities to learn the craft and business of writing. These events are exceptional opportunities to learn, and our events regularly showcase both our own members and nationally known authors, editors, and agents to help League members learn the ropes. I've taken more classes than I can count, and I've given dozens of presentations either to League members, or while representing the League at other events.

Encouragement is critical. The image of an unknown writer typing away in their Fortress of Solitude does nobody any favors. We encourage each other. We cheer at every success, and we commiserate at every setback and delay along this path we share. Let no one tell you that writing is a zero-sum game. One person's success never equates to another person's failure in writing. Through encouragement and shared support, we improve and succeed as a community.

Improvement is a never-ending process. If you think you've learned all there is to know, it's time to dive back into the research because there is always something new to learn. New story structure concepts. New details on characterization. New techniques. New genres. Old ideas transform under new light to expand our toolboxes. Improvement is easier when you share the effort to discover new ideas. Every person in the League has something to share, and every person has something they can learn. Both sharing and learning help us improve.

Finally, we come to goals. Without goals, our every achievement is more a matter of luck than of skill or effort. Some people want to see their name in print. Some want to share copies of their writing with family and friends. Some want a career as an author, editor, agent, or publisher. Set your big goals. With your target set, come to the League to see just what we can do to help you along your road to success, however you define that road.

I've been blessed to be a part of the league, to make new friends, to learn, to achieve goals, and to gain an opportunity to share what I learn along the way. I look forward to seeing others take that same journey.

John M. Olsen

Join us at www.leagueofutahwriters.com